W9-BYX-143

Training for Cross-Country Ski Racing

A Physiological Guide for Athletes and Coaches

**US Ski Team
Sports Medicine Series**

TRAINING FOR CROSS-COUNTRY SKI RACING

A Physiological Guide for Athletes and Coaches

Brian J. Sharkey, Ph.D.
University of Montana

Published under the auspices
of the **United States Ski Team**
by **Human Kinetics Publishers, Inc.**
Champaign, IL 61820

796.93
Sh23t

LIBRARY
ATLANTIC CHRISTIAN COLLEGE
WILSON N C

Production Directors: Kathryn Gollin Marshak and Margery Brandfon
Editorial Staff: Peg Goyette
Typesetters: Sandra Meier and Carol McCarty
Text Layout: Lezli Harris
Cover Design and Layout: Jack Davis

Library of Congress Catalog Number: 83-082292
ISBN: 0-931250-46-3

Copyright © 1984 by Brian J. Sharkey

All rights reserved. Except for use in a review, the reproduction or utilization of this work in any form or by any electronic, mechanical, or other means, now known or hereafter invented, including xerography, photocopying, and record-ing, and in any information storage and retrieval system is forbidden without the written permission of the publisher.

Printed in the United States of America

10 9 8 7 6 5 4 3 2

Human Kinetics Publishers, Inc.
Box 5076
Champaign, IL 61820

To the athletes and coaches
of the United States Nordic Ski Team
and to all the junior, senior, masters,
and citizen racers who cheer them on

DEC 17 1987

P.C. 13.36

87- 1522

DEC 1 1994

Contents

    11 Diet and Performance   129
    12 Environment and Performance   140
    13 Preparation and Performance   150

APPENDIX

        Epilogue   165
    A   The Cross-Country Skiing Fitness Test   168
    B   Cross-Country Skiing Questionnaire   177
    C   Weekly Training Log   180
    D   Dry-Land Training Techniques   182
    E   Back Yard Training Center   184
    F   Muscular Fitness Exercises   186
        Glossary   201
        Recommended Reading   206
        Reference Notes   208
        References   209

Preface

My interest in skiing started in 1964 when I moved west, joined the faculty at the University of Montana, and promptly fell in love with the state, its mountains, and snow. I started with alpine skiing, slipped into ski touring, then gravitated to back-country travel and telemark turns. Sometime around my 40th birthday, as I was looking for a new obsession, I was introduced to track skiing and then to cross-country ski racing. Soon thereafter I was hooked on a sport that offers physical and technical challenges while providing fitness and health benefits.

In 1980 I was honored by a request to join the US Ski Team's Nordic Sportsmedicine Council, an organization dedicated to the continued support and development of cross-country and the other Nordic disciplines. Because of skiing's contributions to fitness and health, the chance to study the extremes of human performance, the intellectual challenge provided by this physiologically complex activity, and my personal interest in skiing as a lifetime sport, I eagerly accepted the opportunity to join in the work of the Council.

The Council attempts to provide US skiers with the medical, nutritional, and sports science support athletes from other countries receive from government-funded sportsmedicine organizations. Our privately supported Council participates in coaching education programs, collects and disseminates information, provides medical support at training camps and major competitions, teaches psychological skills to athletes, conducts biomechanical studies to guide technique, engages in nutritional studies to guide eating behavior, and conducts physiological testing programs to help guide training.

I have studied skiers and the demands of their sport. In addition to lab and field studies I have scoured the research literature for information relative to skiing, attended and conducted symposia on the topic, and engaged in endless discussions with cross-country athletes, coaches, and sports physiologists. This book is an outgrowth of that study.

Written at the request of the US Ski Team and the Sportsmedicine Council, this book is a description of the physiological systems involved in cross-country ski racing along with a systematic plan for their development. The book is intended for use by athletes and their coaches who want to know more about their bodies, the sport, and how to train one for the other. While the content is based on lab and field studies conducted throughout the world, the material is presented in a nontechnical manner for use by the intended audience. Extensive documentation and complex tables and graphs are omitted in favor of communication. Those interested in additional information will find a list of readings and references at the end of the book.

In addition to a discussion of the physiology of skiing and systematic training programs, the book includes other useful information, including ways to monitor overtraining, nutritional guidance, and an extensive appendix with tips on plyometrics and on other dryland training techniques, and fitness tests for cross-country skiers.

ACKNOWLEDGMENT

I am indebted to many people for the ideas and information that make up this book, including Dr. Chuck Dillman and the members of the Nordic Sportsmedicine Council; Jim Page, Nordic Program Director; all the coaches who helped me better understand the sport; ski researchers throughout the world who shared their information and ideas; and Rainer Martens, publisher, colleague, friend, and consistent source of assistance and encouragement.

I also want to acknowledge the wonderful people associated with the sport, people like Jim, John, Mike, Steve, Ruff, Peter, Greg, Joe, Jack, Carol, Marty, Tim, and so many others. I've enjoyed your friendship and learned so much; I only hope I have given something in return.

And finally, I wish to thank U.S. Tobacco Company for its assistance in making this book possible through its funding of the Copenhagen/Skoal US Ski Team Sports Medicine Program.

Brian J. Sharkey
Missoula, Montana

Training for Cross-Country Ski Racing

A Physiological Guide for Athletes and Coaches

Introduction:
The Skier
and the Race

Come with me to a major ski race, where you will learn what it takes to be a successful cross-country ski racer. Upon arrival you'll be dazzled by the splash of colors against the winter landscape. Flags, banners, and racing suits all compete for your attention. From a distance the skiers seem larger than life—lithe but strong, trim but powerful. Up close you'll be surprised to find that ski racers come in all sizes, from diminutive junior girls to stately senior women; from short stocky men to lanky giants. Physique is a poor predictor of success in cross-country racing.

A newcomer to the world of cross-country skiing might expect to see distance runners in racing suits, but that is not the case. While some may consider cross-country a good way for runners to keep in shape during the winter, more commonly, skiers use running and other activities to keep in shape during the summer. Cross-country skiers are lean like runners, but they are also muscular. Their legs must be muscular to carry them over imposing hills; they must develop their arms and shoulders to power them along the track with double pole or diagonal strokes. The body type (somatotype) of the runner is often classified as thin (ectomorph), whereas the skier is a muscular thin person (mesoectomorph) or a thin muscular (ectomesomorph) one.

These distinctions are relevant for recruiting athletes to cross-country ski racing. Although runners have become good skiers, it is the exception rather than the rule. Naive runners who think they can step onto racing skis and blow away the competition with their aerobic power will be unpleasantly surprised. The movements of cross-country skiing are complex and specific and, as you will see in later chapters, develop slowly with years of focused training. This does not mean that runners shouldn't take up cross-country—we're glad to have them. But they are no more likely to achieve success than those who have specific upper body training from kayaking or canoeing or combined arm and leg training from rowing or swimming.

Just as skiers come in many sizes and shapes, they also come in all ages—from tiny tots in the Bill Koch League to masters and senior competitors in citizen races or ski marathons. Many a young athlete has been humbled by a skillful 60-year-old who glides by during a race. Cross-country is a gentle sport that gives more than it takes, so aging athletes can continue their involvement free from the joint and muscle injuries that plague athletes in such sports as distance running and tennis. And while speed and power may decline with age, persistence and resolve do not, leading many older skiers to take on the challenge of citizen races, the Great American Ski Chase, or even the World Loppet Series.

Most racers who achieve success at the national level started skiing when they were very young, some as early as age 2. Like their counterparts in Scandinavian countries, they literally grew up on skis. A few, however, come to skiing rather late in life, usually after a career in another sport. Some start skiing after an injury, others take it up because it represents a new challenge. Because skiers are able to continue high-level competition into their late 30s, a relatively late start is not a major limitation for serious athletes. It does take a number of years for a ski racer to mature in skill and physiological capability, however.

What the spectator cannot see is the time and effort that go into a racer's development. Athletes train hours a day—year-round—to develop the skills and physiological systems used in the race. Most of the training effects are subtle, undetectable to the naked eye. To understand them better, let's crawl inside a skier as he embarks on a race, so we can monitor important systems and relate their importance to performance in ski racing.

THE RACE

We'll join our racer as he skis a portion of the course to simultaneously test his wax, review skills, and warm up for the race. Afterward, it is back to the starting line for that endless wait for the start. Finally, it comes and our racer charges out, double poling and skating furiously across the flat that leads to the first hill. As the racer switches to the diagonal stride to climb the hill, we quickly become aware of his respiration. The rate and depth of breathing are the racer's first clue to the extent of his exertion. Rates of over 40 breaths per minute, combined with a volume of 3 liters of air per breath, are necessary on uphill stretches. The skier will maintain a high level of air intake (ventilation) throughout the race, with some minor relief on long, downhill sections of the course. Because it is linked with muscle metabolism, respiration and the perceptions associated with the removal of excess carbon dioxide provide the experienced racer with the information needed to gauge effort and pace, and still have something left for the last portion of the race.

Less noticeable but no less important is our racer's heartbeat. The heart is the center of the oxygen transport system. The oxygen that enters the blood from the lungs is pumped to the working muscles. The output of the pumping heart, the cardiac output, is the product of the heart rate times the volume pumped each stroke (stroke volume). From the resting value before the warm-up, the heart rate increases at the start of the race to 180 beats per minute or more. On the hills, it may approach the maximal heart rate possible, which averages around 200 beats for a 20-year-old skier. The stroke volume also increases during exercise and, together with the heart rate, pushes the amount of blood pumped per minute five or six times above resting values.

Because the circulatory system is able to restrict blood flow to digestive and other unused organs during vigorous effort, more blood is available to working muscles. This redistribution of blood, together with the rise in cardiac output, combine to increase blood flow to skiing muscles 20 times above resting values. This is particularly important in skiing, where arms and legs often work simultaneously, putting a severe burden on the oxygen transport system. You'll learn much more about the heart, blood, and other components of the oxygen transport system in Chapter 3.

The oxygen entering the lungs is carried in red blood cells by hemoglobin and is pumped by the heart to the muscles. This oxygen is used in oxidative or aerobic (oxygen-using) energy production. A glance into the skier's muscle will typically show a high rate of aerobic energy production, using carbohydrate and some fat in efficient energy pathways. On steep uphill sections, however, the muscles cannot get enough oxygen and are forced to switch to less efficient, nonoxidative (anaerobic) energy pathways and energy sources. These energy sources are in short supply; thus, if our skier miscalculates and pushes too hard, he may become exhausted and have to slow down or even stop. This fatigue could be due to the depletion of energy sources, the buildup of acid by-products (lactic acid) or both. Smart skiers avoid this risk by listening to the signals they receive from their bodies. They avoid excessive or prolonged anaerobic effort, knowing it does little good to lead the first 5 km only to fold before the finish.

As the race continues you may notice our host's temperature rising dramatically. Did he refuse a drink at the last aid station? Is he sweating profusely, losing valuable fluid and not replacing it? Heat stress isn't usually a problem in the winter, but in a long race failure to replace fluids could be a factor. Very long races require additional energy, so our athlete should be taking fluid and some energy every 20 minutes or so.

As the skier approaches the last portion of the race, he is bombarded by sensations of fatigue. Muscle metabolism becomes less efficient, power output is diminished, and stride length decreases. His muscle energy supplies may be depleted, and if he were skiing a marathon, his blood sugar (glucose) might even be down, causing fatigue, confusion, and poor coordination. If the day has been very cold, his muscle temperature may be reduced, resulting in less efficient metabolism and energy production. With fatigue in the muscle and subtle nervous system changes, our athlete may be near exhaustion — until he sees he has but 1 kilometer to go. Then he gets a final bit of help from his tired but game adrenal glands; with a final spurt of adrenalin (epinephrine), he feels a temporary surge of energy and willpower that carries him through to the finish, where he hangs on his poles, spent from the effort.

Within minutes, this frazzled human is showing signs of recovery. A drink, an orange slice, some kind words from coach and teammates and he is ready to do it again — another day. Hours later he is virtually free from the stiffness and soreness that plague runners. He may ski a relay or rest and do a race the following day. Within hours of a race in which he averaged 85% of his capacity for an hour or more, our athlete is almost totally recovered.

SUMMARY

Cross-country skiing is a rapidly growing and changing sport. Large numbers of new US Ski Association memberships go to Nordic skiers. Some are ex-alpine skiers who have been turned off by long lift lines and high prices. Others are attracted by the fitness and health benefits, the new lightweight equipment, or the handsome racing outfits.

Lightweight touring and racing equipment is readily available at a modest cost. Ski touring centers are springing up wherever the snow falls — at least some of the time. And more and more skiers are becoming certified to teach and coach cross-country.

As a result of this interest, ski races are becoming more popular. Thousands line up for the chance to ski the Birkie and other marathons in the Great American Ski Chase. And as more people become involved throughout the world, the standard of excellence rises. All of these changes — the equipment, the courses, the growing number of participants — have altered the physiological demands of the sport.

Today's cross-country ski racer can't be content with a few months of casual preparation. Training starts long before the snow flies with running, roller skiing, and other activities. Racers need more than a good diagonal stride; they must also be ready to shuffle and herringbone steep hills, skate and double pole flats, and tuck the downhill sections. And skiers must improve their strength, endurance, and power with weight training, roller boards, and other devices. This brings me to a major point: cross-country skiing, the sport that was once considered an endurance event, has evolved into a *power-endurance* sport. That's right — power-endurance. In cross-country, you must generate bursts of power and sustain them throughout the race.

Cross-country skiing is an amazing physical challenge. It requires a highly developed endurance capacity, strength in the legs and upper body, power and speed, a well-developed and efficient technique, and the motivation to do your best in training and competition. Not everyone comes equipped to perform well in national competition, but everyone can learn the skills, develop their capacities, and seek their own potential. Along the trail they will be rewarded with an impressive list of health benefits and the satisfactions inherent in the sport. And if runners can get high on their own hormones and become addicted to their sport, imagine how you will feel as you glide along a track that weaves through wood and meadow, with rewarding views of the valley below and the mountain above.

I

THE PHYSIOLOGY OF CROSS-COUNTRY SKIING

Physiology is the study of the body and how it functions. *Exercise physiology* deals with the immediate and long-term effects of exercise on the muscles, organs, and systems of the body. From a physiological point of view, cross-country ski racing is a fascinating sport; it places unusual demands on the body, demands that can only be met after a prolonged period of training.

This section provides the background you will need to understand the physiological effects of training. It outlines the basics of muscle contractions, energy sources and supplies, oxygen transport and utilization, and ends with a consideration of power and endurance.

Muscle: Contraction and Fatigue

After many hours of practice, the movements of cross-country skiing become habits or skills. Repetition of the skill encodes a memory trace in the nervous system, and movements that once required conscious thought become automatic. The nerve cells (neurons) that control the pattern of muscular contractions during complex skiing skills, such as the diagonal stride, originate in the motor control area of the brain. The neurons extend down the spinal cord and pass the message along to the motor neurons that leave the cord to exert direct control on the muscles (Figure 1.1).

This chapter deals with muscles and how they contract. It should help you:

- Identify muscle fiber types and their importance in cross-country skiing;
- Understand the nature and types of muscular contractions;
- Differentiate the cellular effects of specific types of training.

MUSCLE FIBER TYPES

The motor neuron and the muscle fibers it controls is called a motor unit. Each motor unit includes from a few to many hundreds of

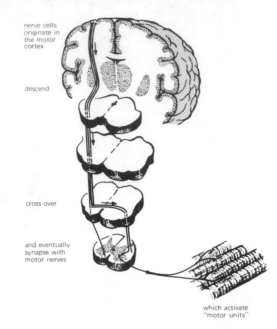

nerve cells originate in the motor cortex

descend

cross over

and eventually synapse with motor nerves

which activate "motor units"

Figure 1.1 The control of muscles.

muscle fibers. Interestingly, each and every muscle fiber in a single motor unit is of the same fiber type—slow or fast. The motor neuron actually dictates the characteristics of the muscle fiber. If the fiber is consistently recruited for slow work, it becomes a slow twitch fiber. If it is recruited for fast contractions, it develops the characteristics of the fast twitch muscle fiber (see Table 1.1).

TABLE 1.1 Characteristics of Muscle Fibers

Characteristics	Slow Twitch or Slow Oxidative	Fast Twitch a or Fast Oxidative Glycolytic (FOG)	Fast Twitch b or Fast Glycolytic (FG)
Average fiber percentage	50%	35%	15%
Speed of contraction	Slow	Fast	Fast
Force of contraction	Low	High	High
Size	Smaller	Large	Large
Fatigability	Fatigue resistant	Less resistant	Easily fatigued
Aerobic capacity	High	Medium	Low
Capillary density	High	High	Low
Anaerobic capacity	Low	Medium	High

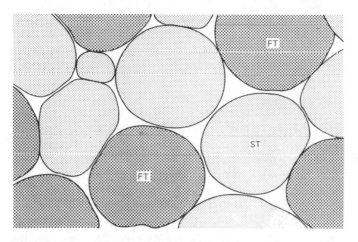

Figure 1.2 Slow and fast twitch muscle fibers intermingle in a cross-section of human muscle.

Most individuals average around 50% slow twitch and 50% fast twitch muscle fibers (35% fast oxidative glycolytic or FOG and 15% fast glycolytic or FG). Studies have shown that world class endurance runners have a high percentage of slow twitch fibers (80%), whereas athletes in the sprints and jumping events usually have more fast twitch fibers. Similarly, cross-country skiers have been found to have greater numbers of slow twitch endurance fibers (63-91%), while downhill skiers tend to have more fast fibers (30-79% ST) (Karlsson et al., 1978). Fiber type certainly has something to do with an athlete's potential for success in cross-country skiing, but it isn't the only thing (Figure 1.2). In fact, other biomechanical factors could override a fiber type disadvantage.

Because the way muscle fibers are used dictates their characteristics, and because we are not able to voluntarily influence the pattern of fiber recruitment, we can say that fiber type is essentially an inherited characteristic. If muscle fiber type is inherited, does that mean training is useless? No, it doesn't. Fiber types can't be changed from slow to fast or vice versa, but fiber *area* can be changed with training. So an athlete with only 50% slow twitch fibers may train hard and achieve well over 50% slow twitch fiber area. Specific training influences specific fibers in specific ways.

Slow twitch fibers contract and relax slowly, but they are very resistant to fatigue. They have energy sources and pathways needed for endurance work. Fast twitch muscle fibers contract twice as fast as the slow ones and produce more force, but they fatigue quickly. The fast oxidative glycolytic (FOG) fibers have somewhat less endurance potential than the slow fibers but far more than fast glycolytic (FG) fibers, which are usually reserved for short, intense bursts of effort. Cross-country ski races are won by athletes who ski fast; therefore, fast twitch fibers are important for success, but no less so than the slow fibers that ensure the endurance required to finish the race.

MUSCLE CONTRACTION

Each muscle contains thousands of spaghetti-like muscle fibers that range from 1 to 45 millimeters in length. The fibers contain the contractile proteins actin and myosin. Muscle fibers shorten and produce movement when the muscle is stimulated by its neuron. The actin and myosin filaments creep along each other via the tiny cross bridges that reach out from the thicker myosin, attach to the actin, and pull like oars. The barely perceptible movement produced in one segment of the muscle is added to the shortening produced along the length of the fiber, resulting in visible motion (Figure 1.3). Because muscles attach to bony lever systems, their movement is multiplied to produce such actions as the kick in cross-country.

Types of Contractions

In most muscular contractions, the muscle shortens. This is called a *concentric* contraction, meaning moving toward the center. The opposite of the concentric contraction is one where the muscle lengthens in spite of the effort to contract, as in letting down a heavy weight. This is called an eccentric contraction, and means moving away from the center. Eccentric contractions are common in sport. For example, in running the contracting thigh muscle (quadricep) is lengthened briefly as it contracts to send the runner forward. The powerful throwing muscles of the arm and chest lengthen momentarily as a javelin thrower prepares to propel the spear. And this same important principle applies to cross-country skiing.

Preload

When a contracted muscle is stretched (eccentric contraction), much of the energy used to stretch the fibers is temporarily stored in the muscle and its tendon. When a *brief* stretch is *quickly* followed by a concentric or shortening contraction, the elastic energy stored in the muscle and tendon can increase the force of the contraction. It has been theorized that the elastic energy stored in a preloaded muscle may account for as much as half of the total work done during a contraction. Utilization of this principle can lead to greater speed of contraction and more power, that is, more force per unit of time. In addition, using stored elastic energy is more energy efficient, allowing more power per unit of energy or the same power for less energy (Thys et al., 1972).

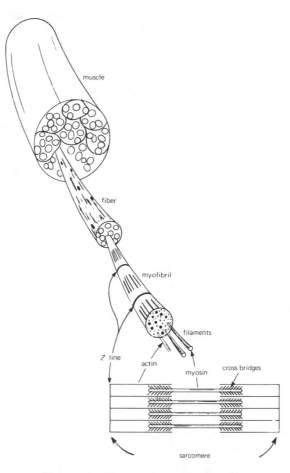

Figure 1.3   The anatomy of a muscle.

Dr. Paavo Komi, physiological advisor to the Finnish National Ski Team, has suggested that preload and elastic recoil can be used in at least four parts of the diagonal stride: poling, trunk flexion, leg extension and ankle extension.* The powerful contraction of the quadricep (thigh) muscle group in the kick can be enhanced by briefly stretching the contracted muscle and then performing the concentric kick. To utilize elastic recoil the brief stretch (preload) must immediately be followed by the contraction. With a slow stretch or a pause, the stored energy will dissipate.

The same principle can be used in the double pole and the single kick-double pole, as well as in the herringbone, uphill shuffle, and skate. Also, it is normally taught as an important part of the step turn.

*Personal communication, 1982.

So if you need more power, or want the same power with less energy expenditure, use preload and elastic recoil in your skiing. Chapter 9 will tell you how.

Force

Since each muscle fiber contracts to the best of its ability (all or none), force is dependent on the number of fibers and motor units involved in a contraction. Slow twitch fibers are recruited for low force output and the larger fast twitch fibers are recruited when more force is required. More frequent nerve impulses can also lead to increases in force. Force output declines with fatigue, so more motor units are required to produce the same force, or the same number of fibers will produce less force.

During the course of a cross-country ski race, stride rate remains fairly constant. But stride length declines as force output drops. The quadricep muscle group on the front of the thigh consists of four major muscles: the three vastus muscles (medialis, intermedius, and lateralis) and the rectus femoris. All four of the quads are involved in extending the leg at the knee. But the rectus, unlike the others, is a two-joint muscle that is also responsible for flexing the thigh at the hip. Because it is involved in the kick and the forward leg swing it is usually the first to fatigue. Both actions of the rectus femoris should be considered in the training program (Figure 1.4).

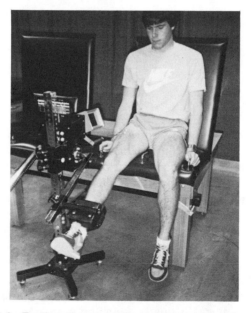

Figure 1.4 Testing the strength and power of leg extensors (quadriceps).

Force-Velocity Relationship

As you can see in Figure 1.5(a), the force produced by a contracting muscle decreases as the rate of shortening (velocity) increases. Power, the rate of doing work ($F \times D$), is maximal when force and

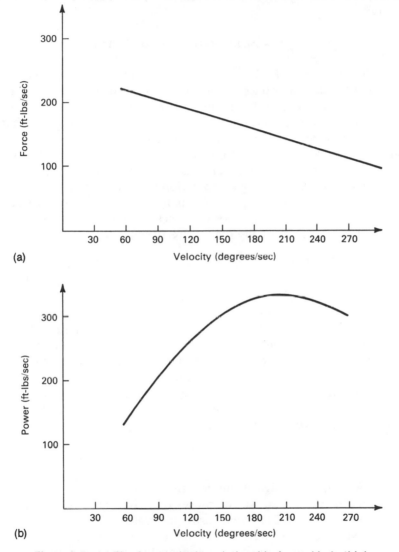

(a)

(b)

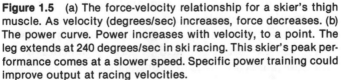

Figure 1.5   (a) The force-velocity relationship for a skier's thigh muscle. As velocity (degrees/sec) increases, force decreases. (b) The power curve. Power increases with velocity, to a point. The leg extends at 240 degrees/sec in ski racing. This skier's peak performance comes at a slower speed. Specific power training could improve output at racing velocities.

velocity are near 35% of their peak values. Excess emphasis on either the speed or force of contraction will sacrifice power and waste energy. Thus, the tempo or stride rate of the diagonal stride should be the optimal combination of force and velocity of shortening that produces the most power and the greatest stride length for the least energy.

$$\text{Speed} = \text{Stride Rate} \times \text{Stride Length}$$

Because optimal values for velocity and force vary with the terrain and because the values are not the same for different muscles or all skiers, it is impossible to provide a formula that tells you how hard and how fast to contract (Figure 1.5b). Each skier must search for that ideal, and change it to meet changing conditions (i.e., snow, wax, grade, fatigue). Lay out a 200-meter course and time repeats with more force at a slower tempo and less force at a faster tempo. You may be able to arrive at the combination that works best for you. If you don't, your body will probably figure it out and choose the one that feels right for the conditions. In fact, in running the natural or comfortable stride is usually the most efficient.

Electromyography (EMG)

When muscles contract, a small electric current is discharged. As in the case of the electrocardiogram and heart muscle, these bioelectric potentials can be recorded from the surface of the skin. When small electrodes are affixed over the active portion of the muscle, EMG recordings indicate when and how much a muscle is involved. The amplitude of the EMG recording indicates the amount of active fibers, and the frequency shows the rate of contraction. The pattern of muscle involvement can be used to compare a less efficient skier to a skilled one. The EMG can also be used to study fatigue patterns, as in the case of the rectus femoris.

FATIGUE

Although a fatigued muscle still attempts to contract all or none, its force declines. All the causes of fatigue are not yet understood, but we can indicate some probable reasons why muscles grow tired. EMG recordings have shown that a fatigued muscle is still getting the message to contract, so it appears that some of the causes of fatigue are within the muscle itself.

Power output declines as intramuscular energy sources decline, acid metabolites increase (lactic acid), energy production drops, and important substances involved in contraction such as calcium are depleted. These factors are not unrelated. Increased acid metabolites brought on by intense effort change the acid-base balance of the cell and reduce the enzymes' rate of energy production, thereby increasing the rate of energy depletion. On the other hand, proper training can increase energy stores, improve energy production, and reduce the rate of lactic acid production.

Another type of fatigue occurs in long distance events, such as a ski marathon. As muscle energy supplies—muscle glycogen—are depleted during several hours of effort, the muscles use more and more blood sugar or glucose for energy. Eventually, the liver runs out of glucose and blood levels start to fall. Since the brain and nervous system rely on blood glucose for energy, the drop in blood sugar is accompanied by signs of impaired nervous function, including poor coordination, confusion, and extreme fatigue. Needless to say, this doesn't do much for form or performance during the last kilometers of the race. A skier capable of skiing 3 minutes per km may drop off to 4 or even 5 minutes per km as blood glucose levels fall. This has obvious implications for diet and in-race feeding, as discussed in Chapter 11.

MUSCLE FIBERS AND TRAINING

In spite of what you may have heard, most of the important effects of training occur in the muscles. In order to better understand training and its effects, let us briefly review some cellular processes and see how they are influenced by training.

Muscle Fibers

Muscle fibers, like all other cells, are encased in a cell membrane that exhibits selective permeability. When it needs something, like glucose, it lets it come in; when it doesn't; it closes its membrane channels. Each muscle fiber has many nuclei along the border. The nuclei carry the hereditary information encoded on the genes, large molecules of DNA. The genetic code is important for the control of vital cell functions such as protein synthesis. A transportation network called the sarcoplasmic reticulum helps distribute materials and messages in the cell.

The fibers also contain the proteins actin and myosin, which are arranged in contractile units. Located in the fluid medium of the fiber are granules of stored energy, muscle glycogen (see Figure 1.6). Small baglike structures called mitochondria, located near the contractile proteins, contain all aerobic or oxygen-using enzymes. The mitochondria are the major energy-producing sites in the muscle. Incidentally, slow twitch fibers have more mitochondria than fast twitch muscle.

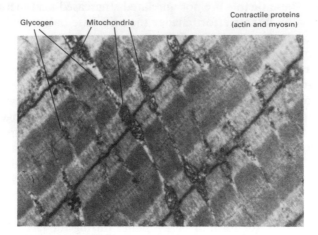

Figure 1.6 Inside the muscle. This microscopic view shows the contractile proteins, numerous mitochondria, and granules of stored glycogen ready to be used as fuel for muscular contrac tions.

Protein synthesis is the function of small granular particles called ribosomes. The ribosomes build protein with the help of RNA. Messenger RNA tells the ribosomes what protein to build, and transfer RNA brings the appropriate building blocks (amino acids) and places them in the growing protein chain. The energy for the process comes from the mitochondria.

Muscle Fiber Training

Although not all the events that occur when a muscle undergoes a training effect can be described, we do know that specific types of training lead to specific changes. Strength training stimulates the muscle to produce more contractile protein, actin and myosin. Endurance training leads to an increase in enzyme protein, specifically the energy-producing aerobic enzymes found in the mitochondria. It also causes an increase in the size and number of mitochondria in the muscle.

The overload of a training bout probably triggers specific protein synthesis, but how the message is transmitted is not understood. Other factors such as the growth hormone, which increases some time after the start of an exercise bout, may also be involved. Whatever the case, we do know that important changes take place in the muscle fiber, and it is clear that the changes are highly related to the type of exercise or training employed. Endurance training increases aerobic enzymes and the size and number of mitochondria. Sprint training increases short-term energy supplies in muscle. Strength training leads to an increase in contractile elements in the muscle. The major effects of training take place in the muscle fibers, and the changes are *specific* to the type of training employed.

SUMMARY

The force output of a muscle is related to its cross-sectional area. Tension develops when the motor nerve stimulates the muscle, leading to the creeping action of actin and myosin. Force output can be increased by preloading the contracted muscle just before it is allowed to shorten.

Fatigue occurs when events within the muscle lead to a diminished force output, and one reason for muscle fatigue is a drop in energy supplies or a reduced capacity to produce energy. Chapter 2 examines the sources and supplies of energy and tells you how to best use the energy you have available.

Energy:
Sources
and Supplies

Muscles won't work without energy. How do you get energy? You get it by eating carbohydrate, fat, and protein foods. The chemical breakdown of these foods releases the energy stored in their molecules. Carbohydrate and fat are the major energy sources for vigorous effort, whereas protein provides the amino acid building blocks needed to build and repair tissue and to synthesize important enzymes and hormones. Although protein can be a source of energy when food intake is low, as in starvation, its role in exercise is not completely understood.

This chapter will help you:

- Understand the energy sources available for muscles;
- Differentiate between aerobic and anaerobic energy pathways;
- Understand the sequence of energy use;
- Determine how training can help you improve energy supplies and pathways, and how it can give you better access to your most abundant source of energy.

The energy that muscles actually use comes from a high energy compound called adenosine triphosphate (ATP). When the nerve impulse stimulates the muscle fiber, ATP splits and releases large amounts of stored energy that causes actin and myosin to slide and muscle to shorten. The resting muscle fiber stores a limited supply of ATP. But if contractions are to last more than a few seconds, stored carbohydrate (muscle glycogen) and fat will have to be broken down to provide a continuous supply of ATP. When muscles can't provide the needed ATP, they fatigue and exert less force.

ENERGY SOURCES

Figure 2.1 illustrates how energy sources are utilized throughout a ski race. For the sake of simplicity, the effects of hills on energy utilization will be temporarily omitted. At the start of the race, stored ATP and its companion compound creatine phosphate (CP) provide the fuel needed. Within seconds, as ATP and CP are quickly depleted, the muscle turns to the pathway that enzymatically breaks down stored glycogen to produce ATP. During the first 30 seconds of effort, it is too soon to have any significant increase in oxygen supply to the muscles. So the energy sources used in this period are nonoxidative or anaerobic. During the first minutes of the race, respiration and circulation adjust to the new demands for oxygen. In time, as the supply equals the demand, ATP comes from the oxidation of carbohydrate and fat, from aerobic enzymes and pathways located in the mitochondria.

The ratio of fat to carbohydrate used depends on the intensity of the effort. Low intensity effort burns mostly fat while the high intensi-

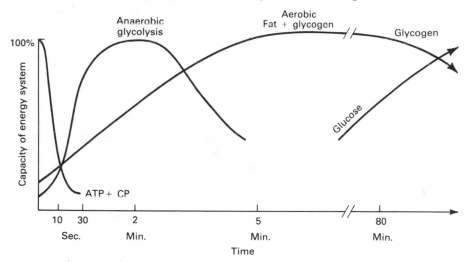

Figure 2.1   Pattern of energy use. As muscle glycogen is used up blood glucose temporarily fills the demand for carbohydrates.

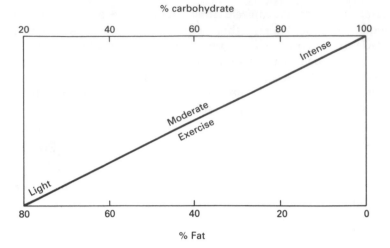

Figure 2.2   Energy utilization during exercise.

ty of a race will burn predominately carbohydrate; work at the maximal oxygen intake is fueled entirely by carbohydrate (Figure 2.2). Fat is poorly supplied with oxygen, so it requires more for metabolism. When oxygen supply is limited, as in vigorous effort, our bodies do the smart thing and switch to muscle glycogen. And, when this begins to run out, our bodies use blood glucose.

ENERGY STORES

An athlete only stores about 4-5 calories of energy in the form of ATP and CP. Glycogen, which is the storage form for glucose molecules, is stored in the muscles and the liver (see Table 2.1). With 20 or more grams of glycogen per kg of muscle, an athlete may have over 1600 calories of carbohydrate energy stored in the muscles. Unfortunately, since it can only be used in the muscle in which it is stored, all the muscle glycogen won't be available to the muscles used in skiing. No more than 80 grams of glycogen are stored in the liver, which releases glucose into the blood whenever blood glucose levels begin to drop. The 80 grams won't go far (320 calories at best), and remember, the brain needs the fuel as much as the muscles.

As you can see, all this adds up to less than 2000 calories, and it isn't all available to the muscles. An athlete burning 20 calories per minute could only ski 100 minutes, and that isn't enough to finish a long race. Clearly, then, fat also must be used to produce ATP in order to keep the skier in motion.

Men on the US Ski Team carry 4-8% of their weight as fat, whereas the women carry 12-17%. Since each pound of fat has 3500

TABLE 2.1   Available Energy Sources

Source	Supply	Energy (Calories)
ATP and CP	Small quantities stored in muscle	5 calories
Carbohydrate		
Muscle glycogen	20 grams (per kg of muscle)	1600 calories
Liver glycogen	80 grams	320 calories
Blood glucose	4 grams	16 calories
Fat	Adipose tissue	30,000-70,000 calories*

*Depends on body weight and % body fat: e.g., 7% fat × 160 lbs = 11.2 lbs fat, 11.2 lbs × 3500 cal/lb = 39,200 calories of fat energy.

calories of energy, men have around 30,000 calories and women over 50,000 calories of energy stored in their several fat depots. Obviously, fat is the most abundant source of energy.

Fat is normally burned during light to moderate activity. You can increase your ability to mobilize and metabolize fat at higher workloads by increasing your aerobic fitness: the ability to take in, transport, and utilize oxygen. Fat will be burned when more oxygen is available and when the enzymes involved in fat metabolism are more concentrated in the mitochondria. Endurance or aerobic energy training accomplishes both these goals and gives you greater access to the abundant fat stores.

ANAEROBIC ENERGY

The anaerobic energy sources in muscle are (a) stored ATP and CP and (b) stored glycogen. ATP and CP, though limited in supply, can be increased in specific types of training. Limited glycogen supplies can be improved with the exercise-diet combination known as carbohydrate loading. It is also possible to improve the enzymatic pathway that extracts energy from glycogen with anaerobic training. This process is called glycolysis or glycogen splitting. And a later discussion will focus on how glycogen utilization can be improved to extract more energy and to use the fuel more efficiently.

Glycolysis

Glycogen is a long chain of glucose molecules. To provide energy, the glycogen first splits to provide six-carbon glucose molecules ($C_6H_{12}O_6$). The glucose moves through a series of enzymatic steps that end up with two three-carbon fragments. When the oxygen supply to the muscle is inadequate, the three-carbon fragments become lactic acid. The breakdown of glucose to lactic acid yields three units of ATP energy. The lactic acid is a by-product that diffuses from the muscle into the blood. Excess lactic acid changes the acid-base balance of the cell and reduces enzyme activity and energy production.

Given the choice between muscle glycogen and blood glucose, the muscle chooses glycogen as an energy source. One unit of ATP is used as glucose enters the muscle, so the net energy gain is one less than for glycogen. But when muscle glycogen levels become depleted the muscle gladly switches to glucose.

Lactic Acid

In light to moderate skiing, which requires mostly slow twitch muscle fibers, the body produces little lactic acid. With more vigorous effort, in which fast-twitch (FOG) fibers are recruited, lactic acid production increases (see Figure 2.3). This is because some of the fibers may not receive enough oxygen and some inefficient ones just aren't very good at aerobic metabolism. In very fast or hard skiing, when you need the help of fast glycolytic fibers, blood lactic acid increases dramatically. The FG fibers are poorly supplied with aerobic enzymes and are best suited for the anaerobic use of glycogen. They should be used sparingly during a ski race because the lactic acid they produce can have adverse effects on performance.

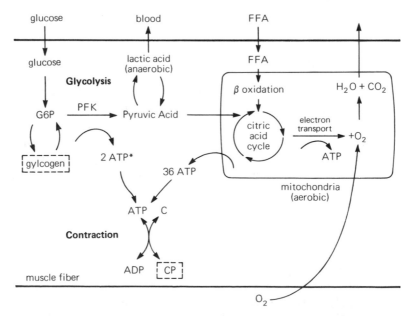

Figure 2.3   Metabolic pathways and the production of energy.

The effect of lactic acid on enzyme activity has already been mentioned. Too much lactic acid and energy production falls. It also prevents the body from using its fat deposits. It inhibits the release of fat from fat storage, forcing even greater reliance on limited muscle glycogen. Lactic acid blocks the action of epinephrine (adrenalin) on fat cells. Normally, epinephrine stimulates the release of fat for use as an energy source. Block the release and the muscle is forced to rely even more on glycogen.

On the good side, some lactic acid might be metabolized for energy during lulls in a race (i.e., downhills, feeding stops). Unfortunately, highly competitive races have few lulls. So lactic acid metabolism for energy is more likely in practice or after the race. Training lowers the lactic acid accumulation at a given rate of exercise, and recent evidence suggests training enhances production of the amino acid alanine instead of lactic acid. The alanine goes to the liver for conversion to glucose, providing energy in a glucose-alanine cycle (Felig, 1977).

AEROBIC ENERGY

When enough oxygen is available, the three carbon fragments from glycolysis move into the mitochondria, where aerobic enzymes extract an additional 36 units of ATP energy. That's right; instead of just three ATPs via anaerobic metabolism, aerobic metabolism produces 3 + 36 or *39* ATPs. So you can see how wasteful anaerobic energy production is and how aerobic pathways conserve your precious energy. If you charge up a long hill early in the race and use glycogen anaerobically, you may run out of fuel before the finish.

Carbohydrate and fat are utilized in aerobic pathways. Carbohydrate fragments from glycolysis (pyruvic acid) enter the mitochondria and are processed in two major pathways — the citric acid cycle and the electron transport system. The final step in the aerobic process involves the union of oxygen, hence the term aerobic or with oxygen. The equation for this union is as follows:

$$C_6H_{12}O_6 + O_2 = CO_2 + H_2O + energy (ATP)$$

Fat is released from fat storage and carried via the circulation to the muscle. Fat fragments (FFA or free fatty acids) enter the mitochondria to be broken into two carbon pieces that join in aerobic pathways with carbohydrate. It has been said that fat burns in the flame of carbohydrate. That means if you run out of carbohydrate (glycogen or glucose), fat metabolism becomes less efficient.

Fat is a wonderful energy source; it has over 9 calories per gram. Unfortunately, because fat requires more oxygen in order to burn, it

87- 1522   LIBRARY
ATLANTIC CHRISTIAN COLLEG
WILSON. N C

cannot be a major source of energy during a ski race. This is especially true at higher altitudes, where the oxygen supply is further limited. For this reason, carbohydrate is the best fuel at altitude.

SUMMARY

Carbohydrate and fat are the principle energy sources we use to produce ATP. Carbohydrate can be processed without oxygen (anaerobically) or with oxygen (aerobically). Aerobic energy production is far more efficient, yielding 39 units of energy (ATP) instead of just three. Fat, the most abundant energy source, can only be used in aerobic pathways. The various pathways and energy sources are selected by a number of cellular controls.

High blood levels of glucose or fat can influence which pathway and fuel the muscle uses. Therefore, if you eat a high glucose meal before a race you will start out using a higher proportion of carbohydrate and could accelerate depletion of muscle glycogen. On the other hand, Dr. Dave Costill has shown that the caffeine in two cups of coffee consumed before an endurance test increases blood fat levels; in other words, caffeine mobilizes the fat. This triggers greater fat usage during the early stages of an endurance event, conserving muscle glycogen. This has not been demonstrated experimentally in a ski race, however, and the prerace adrenalin is probably all you need to mobilize energy. Coffee and other sources of caffeine are commonly used at in-race feeding stations. Caffeine use may soon be regulated in international competition.

Muscle temperature can noticeably affect energy production. For example, warming up the muscles enhances enzyme activity and energy production. And in skiing, proper clothing can be as important as the prerace warm-up. On a cold day the wind chill created by a fast downhill can strip heat from powerful thigh muscles, diminishing energy production. Double-layer racing suits or protection from the wind could help maintain deep muscle temperatures. On a warmer day, too much clothing can cause blood to be diverted from the muscles to the skin to help with heat loss. The result is that the muscle becomes anaerobic and uses energy less efficiently. Proper body and muscle temperatures conserve energy.

ATP levels, oxygen availability, and other factors turn pathways on and off. You need to know how to maximize energy levels via training and diet, and how to best use those sources during the race. The rest of this book is aimed at showing you how.

3

Oxygen: Transport and Utilization

Oxygen is one of the keys to success in cross-country skiing. A steady supply allows you to use more efficient aerobic pathways and more abundant fuel sources. When the working muscles can't get a sufficient supply of oxygen, the body is forced to use inefficient anaerobic pathways and limited energy sources such as ATP, CP, and glycogen.

This chapter will help you:

- Appreciate how the ability to take in, transport, and utilize oxygen dictates exercise capacity;
- Understand the special problems of oxygen transport in cross-country skiing;
- Determine how training to improve oxygen supply and utilization enhances your ability to use fat and conserve muscle glycogen.

OXYGEN

At the beginning of a ski race, oxygen intake does not immediately meet exercise demands. In the first minutes of exercise, as the supply is rising to the occasion, an *oxygen deficit* develops while the

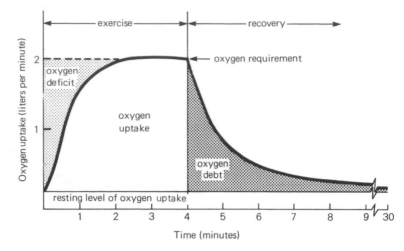

Figure 3.1   Oxygen intake during exercise and recovery.

body relies on ATP, CP, and anaerobic glycolysis for energy (see Figure 3.1). As the respiration and circulation adjust and oxygen intake meets the needs, a relative steady state is achieved,* and exercise can continue as long as the body can meet the fuel requirements. After a race, oxygen intake slowly returns to resting levels. Recovery oxygen intake in excess of resting needs is called the *oxygen debt*. The debt is used to repay the oxygen deficit, replace ATP and CP, remove lactic acid, and help replace liver and muscle glycogen used during the race. Oxygen, then, is the key to prolonged effort. Now, let's see how the oxygen in the air gets from the lungs to the muscles to allow prolonged endurance activity.

Taking in Oxygen

The respiratory system is responsible for getting air into the lungs and oxygen into the circulation (see Figure 3.2). Atmospheric air, containing 20.93% oxygen, enters the lungs when the diaphragm contracts downward, creating an area of lower pressure. When it relaxes we exhale. During vigorous exercise the rib cage is lifted up and out to bring in more air, and the exhale is assisted by contractions of the abdominal and intercostal (between rib) muscles. So breathing during exercise uses more energy and oxygen.

Ventilation. Ventilation (V), the amount of air you move in and out each minute, is the product of respiratory rate or frequency (f) and the volume of air per breath (TV or tidal volume). A typical resting

---

*May be related to the sensation called second wind.

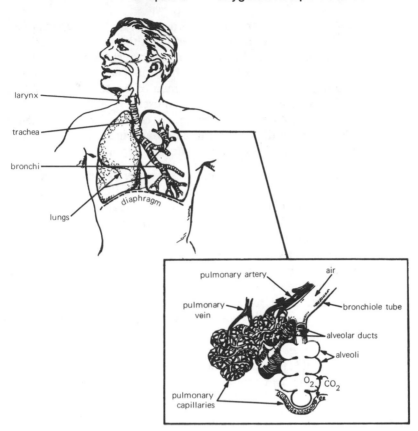

Figure 3.2 Respiration.

value of 6 liters per minute is achieved with a rate of 12 and TV of 0.5 liters, or:

$$V = f \times TV$$

$$6L = 12 \times 0.5$$

During a race, this rate can rise to 40 or 50 breaths per minute times as much as three-fourths of the skier's lung capacity. If the skier has a five-liter vital capacity, that becomes:

$$V = 40 \text{ breaths/min} \times 3.75 \text{ L/breath}$$

$$V = 150 \text{ liters per minute}$$

Neither the vital capacity nor pulmonary ventilation are highly related to endurance performance (except at elevations above 5000 ft).

At lower elevations an athlete with a smaller lung capacity can compensate by breathing more frequently. Although we are able to control the rate and depth of respiration consciously, we usually leave it to the elegant respiratory control mechanism. The system fine tunes air intake to oxygen needs with a minimum of wasted energy. When exercise begins, sensory receptors in the muscles signal a need for increased ventilation. As exercise continues, chemical receptors sense rising levels of carbon dioxide in the blood and use that information for long-term control of respiratory rate and depth.

Breakaway Ventilation. In a progressive exercise test, the ventilation rises as oxygen needs increase (Figure 3.3). Discussed earlier was how the body moves from slow twitch to fast oxidative glycolytic and then fast glycolytic fibers as exercise intensity goes up. Changes in ventilation parallel these fiber recruitment patterns. The rate of increase changes slightly as we move from ST to FOG recruitment. A more pronounced change occurs as FG fibers are recruited in larger numbers. The change is associated with increased anaerobic energy metabolism, lactic acid formation, and consequent carbon dioxide production. The carbon dioxide causes the ventilation to breakaway, that is, to increase at a much higher rate.

This breakaway ventilation can be used as one indication of the anaerobic threshold, that state in which energy is quickly squandered. The increased lactic acid produced in anaerobic exercise is a sign of

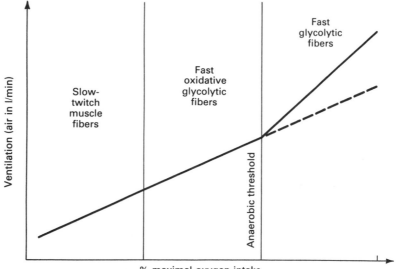

Figure 3.3   Breakaway ventilation and the anaerobic threshold. As exercise intensity increases, FOG and then FG fibers are recruited.

anaerobic metabolism. Lactic acid production increases dramatically because the FG fibers are not well suited for aerobic work. In a race, it is safe to exceed the anaerobic threshold for brief periods—up hills, when passing, or at the finish. Extended stays above the threshold poison the muscle with acid metabolites, overload blood buffer systems with acid, waste limited energy stores, and bring on early exhaustion. The wise competitor becomes familiar with the sensations associated with breakaway ventilation and the anaerobic threshold to avoid these pitfalls.

Diffusion. Oxygen in the lungs' tiny air sacs (called *alveoli*) must cross the alveolar and capillary membranes to get into the blood. The oxygen moves from an area of higher concentration to a lower one. Similarly, carbon dioxide produced in the muscles moves into the blood for removal. Respiration has two major functions: getting oxygen into the body and getting carbon dioxide out. The sensations of distress associated with breathing—the "I ran out of wind" feeling—is not associated with a reduced oxygen level in the blood. Instead, it may indicate a buildup of carbon dioxide. If that happens on a long uphill stretch, relaxing and hyperventilating at the top of the hill may reduce the distress somewhat by "blowing off" the excess carbon dioxide.

Partial Pressure. At sea level, the partial pressure of oxygen (PO_2) in the atmosphere is 760 mm Hg (atmospheric pressure) times 20.93% (percent concentration of oxygen) or:

$$PO_2 = 760 \text{ mm Hg} \times 20.93\%$$

$$= 159 \text{ mm HG}$$

Going up in altitude the percentage of oxygen remains unchanged but the barometric pressure drops. At my lab in Missoula, Montana (elevation 975 meters or 3200 ft), the barometric pressure sits around 680 mm Hg. So the PO_2 is now 680 × 20.93 or 142 mm Hg. At 1980 meters (6500 ft) the PO_2 in the air drops to 125 mm. The PO_2 drops further as air enters the alveoli, because the atmospheric air is mixed with air remaining in the lungs and airways. At sea level, it drops from 159 to 100 mm Hg. And that is the pressure that drives oxygen toward the working muscles, where it can be as low as 20 mm Hg or less.

OXYGEN TRANSPORT

Oxygen transport is a key factor in success in cross-country skiing. It depends on the blood (specifically, red cells and hemoglobin), the heart, and the circulation. In cross-country skiing, both the arms and legs are working simultaneously, and each muscle group needs as much oxygen as it can get. Unfortunately, when arm work is added to leg work, the blood flow and oxygen transport to the legs drop. Thus, it is no accident that world class cross-country skiers have world class oxygen transport systems.

Blood

The typical blood volume of 5 liters constitutes over 7% of body weight for a 70 kg individual. Endurance training can raise blood volume. Red cells number about 5 million per cubic millimeter and constitute about 40-45% of the blood volume or hematocrit. The numbers increase during a sojourn at altitude; hemoglobin averages 16.0 gm per 100 ml blood for men and 14.0 for women. The rise in blood volume, when accompanied by a small increase in hemoglobin, sometimes leads to a condition called "sports anemia." The apparent drop in hemoglobin (per 100 ml of blood) is a normal physiological adjustment, not a cause for alarm. One woman on the national team races well with a hemoglobin value around 13 gm. On the other hand, many young women may be iron deficient and need supplements. Low hemoglobin levels should be followed by iron tests to determine if supplements are needed.

Each gram of hemoglobin carries up to 1.34 milliliters of oxygen, so someone with more hemoglobin should have an advantage in oxygen transport. A skier with 15 grams of hemoglobin can carry 15 grams $\times$ 1.34 milliliters O_2 or 20.1 ml oxygen in each 100 cc unit of blood. However, the body may be able to adjust for lower hemoglobin values by pumping more blood. This is possible because blood with less hemoglobin is less viscous, less difficult to pump.

The importance of the hemoglobin level is still being investigated. In the meantime, you can keep up your iron or hemoglobin levels by eating a mixed diet with adequate calories. This diet must include meat, fish, and poultry, because our bodies tend to absorb iron more readily from animal sources. And if your diet isn't enough to maintain an adequate iron level, an iron supplement should take care of the problem.

Heart

The heart of the endurance athlete is often, but not always, larger than that of less active individuals. Enzyme studies of animal heart muscle do not show dramatic changes with endurance training. And the thickness of the wall of the left ventricle, the chamber responsible for pumping blood throughout the the body, is not enlarged in endurance runners. Echocardiograms, sonar-like studies of heart walls and chambers, reveal no enlargement (hypertrophy) of the vessel walls. What does change is the volume of blood contained in the left ventricle when it fills during its brief rest (diastole). The truly signifi-

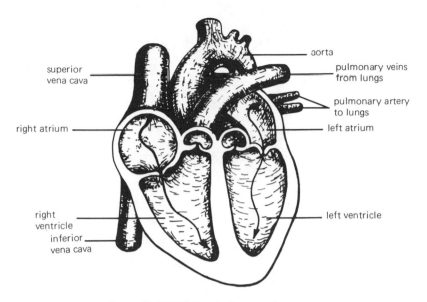

superior
vena cava

aorta

pulmonary veins
from lungs

pulmonary artery
to lungs

right atrium

left atrium

right
ventricle

left ventricle

inferior
vena cava

Figure 3.4   The heart: A muscular pump.

cant change in the trained heart is a larger *end diastolic volume* of the left ventricle. Is it larger because the heart rate is slower in the trained individual (see Figure 3.4), allowing more time to fill, or is the heart rate slower due to the greater volume of blood pumped each beat?

Cardiac Output. The amount of blood pumped each minute, the cardiac output (CO), is the product of the heart rate (HR) times the stroke volume (SV), which is the amount of blood pumped each beat or stroke of the pump.

$$CO = HR \times SV$$

At rest cardiac output is about 5 liters (72 beats per min x 70 ml/beat). The trained athlete accomplishes this output with a lower heart rate and a higher stroke volume (50 bpm x 100 ml). During maximal effort, the cardiac output can increase 5 to 7 times in an endurance athlete, with the highest values ever recorded (38 liters) registered on cross-country skiers. Figure 3.5 illustrates the pattern of response during exercise and the effects of training on the heart rate and stroke volume.

Maximal heart rates are often somewhat lower in endurance athletes than in nonathletes. Average maximal heart rates are plotted in Figure 3.6. The shaded area indicates plus or minus 12 beats (one standard deviation), and includes 68% of the population. Some individuals have rates two or even three standard deviations above or

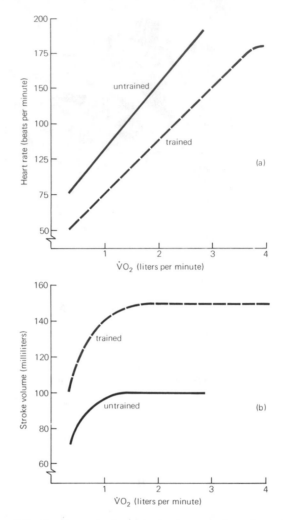

Figure 3.5   Cardiac output = heart rate × stroke volume. These figures show the relationship of exercise intensity (oxygen intake or $\dot{V}O_2$) to heart rate (a) and stroke volume (b), before and after training.

below the average. So with an average of 196, you could find someone with a maximal rate as low as 160 or as high as 232. In Chapter 7, you will learn how to determine your own maximal heart rate.

During exercise of increasing intensity, the heart rate rises toward the maximum in a straight line or linear fashion (Figure 3.5). The relationship between heart rate and factors such as oxygen uptake and caloric expenditure is so good, you can use the heart rate to predict them or to guide the intensity of training.

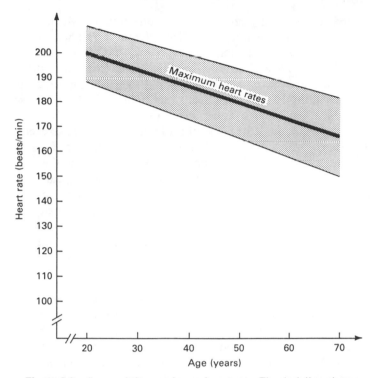

Figure 3.6 Age and the maximum heart rate. The dark line shows the decline with age. The shaded area represents 68% of the population; that is, 68% of all 20-year-olds have maximum rates between 188 and 212. A few have maximum rates under 170 or above 230. (Data from Cooper et al., 1975.)

Stroke volume also increases with exercise, but in a different way (see Figure 3.5). It achieves a near maximal value at a moderate workload and changes little thereafter. The amount of blood pumped per beat is a function of the vigor of contraction and the amount that fills the left ventricle. Put more in and you get more out. So events that aid diastolic filling will help the stroke volume, cardiac output, and oxygen transport. Trained athletes, then, have lower heart rates, which allow more time for filling. Their bodies also are better able to redistribute blood; specifically, blood is diverted from digestive and other organs for use by the working muscles, aiding venous return or the flow of blood back into the heart. And constriction of veins keeps blood from pooling, which also aids venous return and cardiac output.

Earlier I asked, does the athlete's heart beat at a slower rate because stroke volume is greater, or is stroke volume greater because of a slower heart rate? Swedish physiologist Dr. Bengt Saltin (1977) conducted a fascinating study on this question in which subjects trained one leg while keeping the other sedentary. The heart rate was higher when the untrained leg was exercised, indicating support for peripheral (local muscle) control of heart rate. It appears that tiny nerve endings in muscles send impulses to the cardiac control center in the brain, calling for a faster heart rate. The trained muscle sends fewer impulses, allowing a slower heart rate, more filling time, and a greater stroke volume. Chemical stimuli within the muscles excite the nerve endings, which means that when you do endurance training of the muscles used in skiing, the changes that take place in the muscles allow a slower heart rate at a given work load and a greater stroke volume. The total effect is a far more efficient heart and oxygen transport system, in spite of the fact that few dramatic changes take place in the heart itself. It seems that some of the so-called cardiovascular benefits of exercise are really secondary to changes in the muscles.

Circulation

The final part of the oxygen transport system delivers oxygenated blood and fuel to the working muscles. Arteries branch to smaller arterioles and eventually capillaries, where oxygen leaves the blood and enters the muscle. Blood flow in the capillary network is controlled by the arterioles. They constrict and limit blood flow in the resting muscle. When the muscle begins to exercise it quickly uses up any available oxygen. This causes the arterioles to dilate and allow more blood to enter the muscle. When arterioles in a large muscle open, blood pressure drops and the pressure receptors in the arteries sense this. They signal the need for more pressure and the cardiac control center calls for a faster and a more vigorous heart beat.

Cross-country skiers have a greater capillary density in their endurance-trained muscles, providing more efficient oxygen transport. This increase in capillarization does not occur in untrained muscles or with other types of training (such as strength training). It is a specific response to a specific type of training.

OXYGEN UTILIZATION

Chapter 2 outlined some of the effects of endurance training on muscles, where the oxygen is actually utilized. This section will be but a brief summary.

Myoglobin, the hemoglobin-like compound in the muscle that helps grab oxygen and put it to work, is increased with training. The size and number of mitochondria increase, as do the activity or concentration of important aerobic or oxygen-using enzymes in the mitochondria. Enzymes responsible for fat metabolism increase in activity.

Aerobic enzyme activity can double after 12 weeks of training, and with an appropriate diet, muscle glycogen levels can be raised. More fat is stored in the trained muscle, ready for use as a fuel.

All of these changes enhance the ability of muscle to utilize oxygen in efficient, high-yield energy pathways. This reduces the reliance on anaerobic metabolism. Greater fat utilization conserves limited glycogen stores and provides an almost endless supply of energy—at least as much as is needed for any ski marathon in the world.

Arterio-venous Oxygen Difference

One indication of oxygen utilization in a muscle is the drop in oxygen concentration between artery and vein:

$$A - \overline{V}O_2 \text{ diff}$$

Sport physiologists use this measurement to study a skier's ability to utilize oxygen, and have found that well-trained muscle can extract more oxygen than untrained. Therefore, there is a bigger drop between the arterial and venous oxygen content. The well-trained skier can wring more oxygen from a unit of blood, an important factor when blood supply becomes limited, as it does when a cross-country skier combines vigorous arm and leg work in the diagonal stride (Figure 3.7).

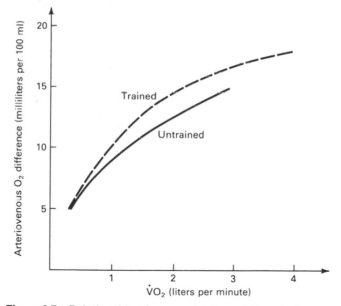

Figure 3.7   Relationship of oxygen intake and the arteriovenous O_2 difference. As work load increases, the extraction of oxygen increases. Trained muscles are better able to utilize the oxygen carried in the blood.

SUMMARY

This chapter has shown how the elements of aerobic fitness—oxygen intake, transport, and utilization—contribute to performance in skiing. The information provides additional reasons for emphasizing specificity in ski training. The major effects of endurance training are found in the trained muscles. Heart rate and stroke volume are dictated, in part, by impulses arising from the muscles. Some of the effects of exercise on the heart, then, are specific to the type of training and muscles used.

This chapter also points out, in a sport that involves simultaneous arm and leg work, the importance of the capacity of the oxygen transport system to success. While studies show that the system can be enhanced via training—especially during the developmental years—there are undoubtedly some genetic limitations to this development. At present we are unable to predict the limits to that development.

The ability to get air into the lungs and then into the blood is not a limiting factor in vigorous exercise for the individual with a healthy respiratory apparatus. However, at elevations above 1500 meters the partial pressure of oxygen does begin to pose problems, and respiration can impose a limit on maximal performance. Therefore, athletes with respiratory problems such as asthma and allergies need special help so they can train and race up to their capacity.

Cross-country ski training will improve oxygen transport in many ways. It will produce increased blood volume and total hemoglobin as well as improved cardiac output (increased end diastolic volume). It will also allow better blood distribution and greater capillary density. Unfortunately, these factors cannot continue to change with years of training. Each person eventually reaches some maximum dictated by heredity or perhaps the time one can devote to training. So cross-country performances will always be limited by oxygen transport to a degree. This limitation will be considered in more detail in Chapter 4.

Performance: Endurance and Power

Once considered an endurance sport, cross-country skiing has become a power and endurance sport. The equipment, the courses, and even the skiers have changed to make this always demanding sport even more awesome in its physical requirements.

This chapter explores the dimensions of endurance and power and tells you how to improve them. It should help you:

- Understand the factors that limit endurance;
- Determine the components that contribute to power;
- Describe how specific types of training contribute to endurance, power, and performance in cross-country ski racing.

ENDURANCE

In physiological terms,* endurance—the ability to persist, to withstand hardship and stress—is a composite of the following components:

- Maximal oxygen uptake (aerobic fitness)
- Anaerobic threshold

*Psychological components of endurance involve motivation, commitment, and other factors.

- Energy utilization
- Efficiency

Let's consider these components individually.

MAXIMAL OXYGEN INTAKE

As described in Chapter 3, the maximal O_2 or aerobic fitness is defined as the ability to take in, transport, and utilize oxygen. It is measured in a progressive work test that terminates when the subject becomes exhausted and can't continue, or when the oxygen uptake plateaus or doesn't increase with a higher workload. For skiers, the best test of oxygen intake is on skis. However, because on-snow tests are so difficult to set up and control, we utilize lab tests designed to involve the muscles and movements of skiing. To better understand oxygen intake in skiing we use separate tests for the arms, the legs, and the arms and legs (combined).* The maximal oxygen intake is usually measured in liters of oxygen (aerobic capacity). Because the value is related to body size, however, it is divided by weight in kilograms to get the intake per unit (kg) of body weight (aerobic power). Both measures are relevant in cross-country skiing.

Tests conducted on junior and senior members of the US Ski Team provide diagnostic information to help guide training programs (Sharkey & Heidel, 1981). The maximal oxygen intake (legs or combined) is one useful measure of a skier's potential. World class skiers range from the low 70s to the 80s (ml/kg/min) for men and the 60s to 70s for women. The oxygen intake score will increase with training up to a point, when eventually the value plateaus. Performance, however, doesn't plateau because other endurance factors can still be improved.

Arms versus Legs

A comparison of arm versus leg values indicates the extent to which upper body endurance has been developed. While in untrained individuals the arms seldom exceed 70% of leg values, our studies show that highly trained skiers can achieve 85% of leg scores. Thus, if a skier has a leg score of 70 ml/kg/min, arm values should approach 85% × 70 = 59.5 ml, a value high above the average *total body* score for an untrained individual (see Figure 4.1a). Experience has shown that highly motivated athletes can approach this standard and that the improvements are reflected in skiing performance.

---

*Test values in liters of oxygen (aerobic capacity) are highly related to body size, so we divide by weight in kilograms to get oxygen intake in milliliters of oxygen per kilogram of body weight per minute (aerobic power). However, the value in liters is also important because it describes the capacity of the oxygen transport system.

Figure 4.1 Maximal oxygen intake tests. (a) Dr. Rik Washburn monitors oxygen intake and heart rate while Mik Smith adjusts the resistance during an arm test. (b) Here the author encourages maximal effort in a combined arm and leg test.

Studies show that arm muscles are at least as trainable as those in the legs. The differences in oxygen intake scores merely reflect differences in muscle mass. Until recently, skiers didn't engage in as much arm endurance training. But changes in technique call for a greater contribution from the upper body, requiring additional emphasis on aerobic training of the arms and upper body.

Combined versus Legs

Combined (arms and legs) oxygen intake scores have also been compared with leg values to see if the larger muscle mass involved in the combined test yields a higher oxygen intake score. Put another way the question becomes, can the oxygen transport system meet the combined arm and leg needs during simulated skiing?

Studies of arm, leg, and combined exercise suggest that the oxygen intake ability of the arms limits the combined test score (Secher et al., 1974). Our data on US Team athletes supports that contention. Those with high arm values are able to exceed leg scores in the combined test, whereas those with low arm scores cannot (Figure 4.1b). Bergh (1976) confirmed the concept when he reported that combined oxygen intake scores fall below leg values when the arms are asked to contribute more than 40% of the total work. So it appears that oxygen intake during combined arm and leg work is limited by the aerobic ability of the arms. There will be more about arm and leg work shortly (Figure 4.2).

Oxygen Intake and Endurance

Before proceeding any further, we should consider just how important oxygen intake is to endurance. Studies on skiers, runners, and

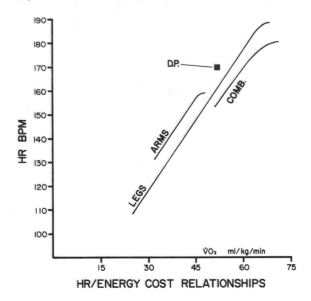

HR/ENERGY COST RELATIONSHIPS

Figure 4.2 Maximal oxygen intake for arms, legs, and combined arm and leg work. Data for a classified skier indicate an arm oxygen intake score that is 70% of the leg value. The combined arm and leg score was slightly higher than the legs alone test, which could suggest a well-developed oxygen transport system. This skier would profit from more arm endurance work. Note that the heart rate-oxygen intake relationship is different for the three tests, and that the double pole (DP) test followed the pattern of the arm test.

animals confirm a significant correlation between endurance performance and the maximal oxygen intake. The correlation usually doesn't account for more than 50% of the relationship, however, leaving the other half of performance unexplained. The reason for this is relatively simple. The maximal $\dot{V}O_2$ score is a rather gross measure of the body's ability to take in, transport, and utilize oxygen during maximal effort. It falls short for several reasons:

1. Performance in skiing involves much more than aerobic ability. It also includes other physiological factors, as well as equipment, technique, and motivation.
2. Oxygen intake in the specific muscles used in skiing is more highly related to performance.
3. Skiers don't perform at maximal levels; maximal tests are not the best predictors of endurance performance.

Animal studies confirm the high relationship between the *muscles'* oxygen intake ability and endurance performance, with muscle oxygen intake predicting 85% of endurance performance. It is possible for some muscles to double their aerobic capabilities while the total body maximal oxygen intake rises only 14% (Davies, Packer, & Brooks, 1981). So although the maximal oxygen intake test has diagnostic value, it should not be viewed as a predictor of—or limit to—success in cross-country skiing.

Mode of Testing. Oxygen intake values vary according to the mode of testing. Treadmill tests are often as much as 7% higher than bicycle tests, except on cyclists who score a bit higher on their specific test. Skiers have been tested while uphill striding, bounding, and running, and the running tests usually yield higher scores, although fast walking and bounding seem related to the movements of the sport. We need tests that will reflect the effects of training on ski performance and we need a device to allow the detailed study of skiing in the laboratory environment.

Ski Treadmill. Although several devices attempt to simulate the movements of cross-country, none are close enough for laboratory study (Figure 4.3). However, Sven Wik of Colorado is currently working on a skiing treadmill that may do the job. The first version of the skimill provides a close approximation of the movements, using standard skis and poles. With technical modifications now underway, we may soon be able to conduct extensive physiological and biomechanical tests in the laboratory. Tests underway at Dr. Art Dickenson's Human Performance Lab at the University of Colorado show that the skimill is an effective tool for the measurement of oxygen intake dur-

Figure 4.3   (a) A skiing simulator. The SKI IMIT is manufactured in Norway. (b) A ski treadmill (skimill). Shown with the inventor, Sven Wik, this prototype is being evaluated for ski research by Dr. Art Dickinson and his colleagues at the University of Colorado.

ing skiing, and that treadmill running and skimill values for oxygen intake and anaerobic threshold closely agree (Weltman, Dickenson, & Burns, 1982).

Oxygen Transport versus Utilization

As we have said, the ability to take in oxygen isn't considered a limit to endurance performance. Thus, we can consider oxygen intake to be a function of

$$O_2 \text{ intake} = HR \times SV \times a - \bar{v} O_2 \text{ difference}$$

In this equation HR and SV (or cardiac output) are central circulatory factors involved in oxygen transport, and the arteriovenous oxygen difference ($a - \bar{v} O_2$ difference) represents oxygen utilization in the muscles.

My colleagues and I have performed cardiac output studies (CO = HR × SV) on classified ski racers to better understand how oxygen transport and utilization relate to performance. We measured cardiac output using the carbon dioxide rebreathing technique, and divided the measured cardiac output by heart rate to determine the stroke volume. Cardiac output can also be described by the equation

$$CO = \frac{\text{Oxygen intake}}{a - \bar{v}\ O_2 \text{ difference}}$$

Thus, by knowing oxygen intake and cardiac output we are able to determine the arteriovenous oxygen difference, the amount of oxygen that the muscles extract from each unit of blood. These measurements allow us to see if oxygen transport or utilization limit performance during combined arm and leg work that simulates cross-country skiing.

As you might expect, cardiac output is related to performance in skiing. In fact, since cardiac output and oxygen intake are highly related (Figure 4.4), a relationship to performance is not surprising. The best skier in a sample of classified racers had the largest cardiac output (32 liters) and stroke volume (165 ml). He also scored highest in oxygen intake (72 ml/kg/min or 5 L/min) (Figure 4.5). Skiers with a lower cardiac output and stroke volume were able to compensate somewhat during submaximal work by extracting more oxygen from the blood, using up an important oxygen reserve. But at higher work loads, their muscles were forced to work anaerobically. Data on world class skiers from the US and those from other countries indicate cardiac output values above 38 liters and stroke volumes approaching 200 ml per beat. These values stand among the highest ever measured.

Arms and Legs. Related research on arm cranking and cycling shows that in *untrained* subjects, stroke volume relates more to performance of leg exercise whereas oxygen utilization (a − $\bar{v}$ O$_2$ difference) is more related to work with the arms. After training, the central circulatory oxygen transport factor, the stroke volume, was the major limitation for both types of exercise. Thus, oxygen utilization may limit performance in the early stages of arm training, but as training progresses oxygen transport becomes more important (Boileau, McKeown, & Riner, 1981).

In another cycling study, Secher et al. (1974) added arm work to leg work or vice versa while measuring oxygen intake, cardiac output, muscle blood flow, and lactic acid. In fit but not highly trained subjects, the addition of arm to leg work caused a decrease in leg blood flow and an increase in oxygen utilization by leg muscles. The demands of combined arm and leg work limit blood flow to muscles,

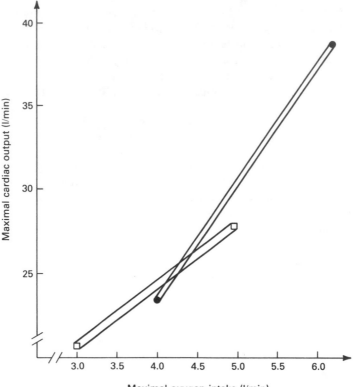

Figure 4.4 Cardiac output and oxygen intake. The relationship of maximal oxygen intake to maximal cardiac output in elite cross-country skiers (•) and those with less training (□). Part of the difference in the relationship may be explained by inherited differences in heart size. Cross-country skiing requires high cardiac output and oxygen transport capabilities.

which adjust by increasing the amount of oxygen they extract from each unit of blood. When the muscles are not sufficiently trained to utilize oxygen or when blood flow becomes inadequate, the muscles work anaerobically, producing lactic acid and fatigue.

Body Weight. Dr. Ulf Bergh, an exercise physiologist with a long history of service to the Swedish National Team, has compiled data on world class skiers that provide an interesting insight into the relationship between oxygen intake and performance (Bergh, 1982). Among successful male skiers, those with larger body weight (over 80 kg) were able to achieve success with oxygen intake scores in the 70s (ml/kg/min). The smaller skiers typically scored higher per kilogram of body weight (over 80 ml/kg/min). Although one factor in this relationship may have been the value of weight on the downhills, it is also

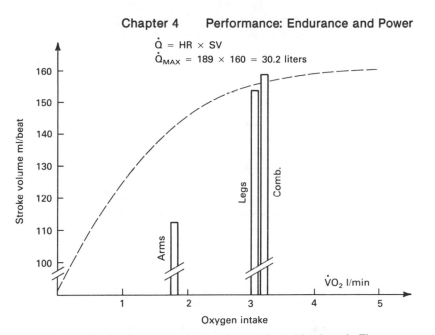

Figure 4.5 Stroke volume in arm, leg, and combined work. The slightly higher stroke volume during combined arm and leg work explains why the maximal heart rate (see Figure 4.1) is slightly lower during combined work. The low arm value is caused by the pooling of the blood in the legs during the arm test.

likely that heavier skiers weighed more partly because they carried more upper body muscle, and muscle contributes to performance. So the oxygen intake in milliliters per kilogram of body weight doesn't tell the entire story about success in skiing.

Summary

Oxygen uptake, expressed in liters of oxygen or in milliliters per kilogram of body weight, is related to performance in skiing (see Figure 4.6). Some larger world class skiers have high scores in *liters* but more modest scores per kilogram of body weight. This can be explained by the fact that, unlike in running, extra weight does not impose a handicap on the skier. The extra weight on world class skiers is primarily upper body muscle that contributes power to the performance. A better predictor of endurance is the muscle's ability to utilize oxygen, as determined by mitochondria and aerobic enzymes.

Because the arms seldom receive the endurance training given the legs, they tend to limit combined arm and leg performances. Training should focus on the improvement of the aerobic or oxygen-utilizing capabilities of the arms, especially if arm scores are below 80% of leg values. Thereafter, combined arm and leg training should be used to ensure maximal development of the oxygen transport and utilization systems.

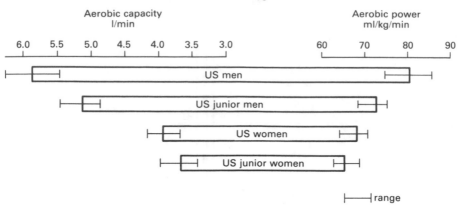

Figure 4.6 Aerobic capacity and aerobic power for elite junior and senior men and women. Power scores (ml/kg/min) vary according to level of training and body weight.

In the meantime, the best thing to do is to utilize talents that already exist. Ask too much of the arms and the entire system fails. Don't put too much into the arms during a race and go under before the finish. Instead, use them judiciously so they will be there all the way to the finish line.

ANAEROBIC THRESHOLD

The anaerobic threshold (AT) marks the point at which lactic acid accumulation exceeds 4 mmoles (see Figure 4.7) and indicates the transition from predominately aerobic to anaerobic metabolism. Because aerobic energy production is far more efficient than anaerobic, it also signals a significant limit to continued performance. Training at or near the anaerobic threshold helps the aerobic abilities of fast oxidative glycolytic fibers, raising the intensity of effort that can be sustained aerobically. For example, a skier with a maximal O_2 of 70 ml and an AT of 70% (of maximum) can "cruise" at an oxygen uptake of 49 ml/kg/min (70 × 70 = 49), or about 270 meters per minute.* Raise the AT to 80% and the cruising speed increases to 56 ml (70 × 80) or 320 meters per minute.

Skiers on the US team registered a threshold between 80 and 92% of their maximal oxygen uptake (see Table 4.1). Highly trained endurance athletes should approach 90% as the season draws near.

*The exact cost of skiing depends on the grade, snow conditions, wax, and technique utilized (i.e., double pole vs. skate, diagonal vs. double pole-single kick), as well as the level of skill.

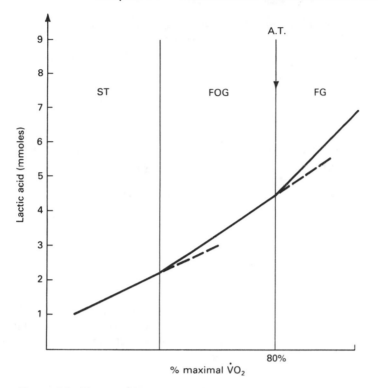

Figure 4.7 The anaerobic thresnold (AT). As exercise intensity ($\dot{V}O_2$) increases, we begin to recruit more FOG fibers. When the effort demands more FG fibers, more lactic acid is produced. The point where lactic acid production begins to climb faster than it can be removed is called the anaerobic threshold.

TABLE 4.1   Maximal Oxygen Intake Data for Elite Skiers†

	Senior		Junior		Nordic
	Men	Women	Men	Women	Combined
N =	3	4	6	7	4
Age	25.3	22.3	18.2	17.4	17.5
Ht (ins)	71	63.7	70.5	64.5	66.6
Wt (lbs)	180	127.0	153.0	124.2	133.8
$\dot{V}O_2$ arms (ml/kg/min)	60.6	40.1	48.3	41.3	47.7
$\dot{V}O_2$ legs	70.8	60.5	63.5	57.3	64.2
$\dot{V}O_2$ comb*	70.3	61.2	64.1	57.5	63.8
Arms/Legs %	85.5	66.3	76.5	72.3	74.2
Comb/Legs %	99.2	101.2	100.4	100.3	99.3

*Combined arms and legs
†From Sharkey and Heidel, 1982

This is accomplished by training at or slightly above the anaerobic threshold, which is a demanding stage of training and should be preceded by weeks of lower intensity aerobic training (see Chapter 8).

Arms versus Legs

Individuals who have not engaged in specific arm endurance training will have an arm anaerobic threshold of about 50% of the arm maximum value. Because muscle fiber composition and oxygen uptake ability are similar in arm and leg muscles, we should expect the arms to approach the same AT as the legs (90% for endurance athletes). Indeed, preliminary studies on elite skiers working on the ski-mill show that the AT during simulated skiing is similar to that measured while running on a treadmill (Weltman et al., 1982).

Summary

Oxygen uptake goes up with training but eventually reaches a plateau dictated in part by genetic factors such as muscle fiber type. Thereafter, specific training will raise the anaerobic threshold and provide continued improvements in endurance performance (Figure 4.8). Eventually, the AT also plateaus. From then on, improvements in endurance are largely the product of careful energy utilization and improved skiing efficiency (technique).

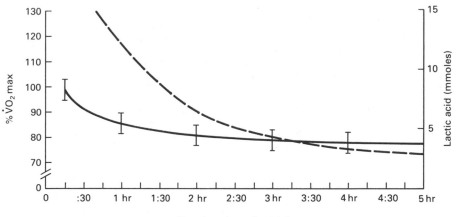

Figure 4.8   The relationship of race duration to percent maximal oxygen intake that can be sustained (solid line) and postrace lactic acid accumulation (dashed line). Note that the lactic acid drops below 4 mmoles (anaerobic threshold) after 3 hours of ski racing. Athletes with higher thresholds can sustain higher work rates (% of VO$_2$ max) and those with lower thresholds are forced to work at lower rates. (Adapted from Bergh, 1982, and Daniels, Fitts, and Sheehan, 1978.)

ENERGY UTILIZATION

Endurance can be enhanced by careful energy storage and utilization.

Energy Storage

Muscle glycogen holds the key to high intensity endurance performances. In lab studies, the best endurance performances have always been performed when muscle glycogen stores were highest. Glycogen storage is dependent on two factors: (a) glycogen depletion, and (b) high carbohydrate diet. While glycogen becomes depleted over the course of a long workout or race, depletion takes place faster when the effort is intense. So long, hard workouts are more likely to deplete glycogen levels in skiing muscles than shorter or easier ones.

The return of glycogen to the muscle is triggered by the activation of an enzyme, glycogen synthatase. Give the muscle glucose and it will store it as glycogen. That means dietary carbohydrate intake should be about 60% of your total daily calories. Complex carbohydrates like potatoes, rice, corn, beans, whole grain breads, and pasta and even some junk food like donuts and candy will enable you to do so. Fruit sugar or fructose is good but not as effective as other carbohydrates for glycogen loading. For details on carbohydrate loading, see Chapter 11.

Energy Use

In a long race, the way you use energy could mean the difference of many minutes at the finish. The trick is to try to use as much fat as possible, conserving glycogen so it lasts the entire race. Athletes who don't carbohydrate load are probably good at this. Once again, there is more on energy use, pre- and in-race feeding in Chapter 11.

EFFICIENCY

Elite skiers are more efficient than most citizen racers. They can ski a certain speed (e.g., 300 meters/min) using 5-10% less energy. They become efficient after many hours and years of practice under the guidance of a perceptive coach. They eliminate extraneous movements and fine-tune their skill to produce the most speed with the least effort.

Experienced skiers get the most from each phase of skiing. They select the most effective form of propulsion for the terrain and snow conditions. They maintain momentum or make up time where others lose it — in transitions, corners, on uphills, and downhills. Years of practice allow them to get the most from poor tracks or a marginal wax job, whereas less experienced skiers flail away, using an unproductive approach to the conditions. Elite skiers also use more efficient energy pathways and fat, the more abundant fuel.

We could teach efficient skiing more quickly if we could monitor energy expenditure and speed and provide immediate feedback to the skier. Because field methods for measuring oxygen intake (Figure 4.9) are cumbersome, time consuming, and less accurate than modern metabolic measurement systems, on-snow measurements are not the only answer. We need a laboratory device to accurately simulate the skills of skiing. A skiing treadmill may someday help coaches and

(a)   (b)

(c)

Figure 4.9 Field measurements of oxygen intake. (a) A breathing valve directs expired air into a lightweight collection system. After a timed test (b), the volume of expired air and the oxygen content are measured via an oxygen analyzer (c). These techniques are also used for on-snow measurements.

sports scientists work together to teach as much efficiency in days or weeks as it now takes months or years to develop.

Skiing skills take years to develop, partly because the athlete can only spend about 4 to 5 months of each year on the snow. As roller skis continue to improve and when lab devices become available, the mastery of technique may occur more rapidly. In the meantime, the next best answer is a good coach, polarvision or a video recorder, and a summer on the nearest glacier.

POWER

Power has emerged as an essential ingredient in the physiological recipe for success in cross-country ski racing. It is described by the formula:

$$\text{Power} = \frac{F \times D}{t}$$

$$\begin{aligned} \text{where } F &= \text{force} \\ D &= \text{distance} \\ t &= \text{time} \end{aligned}$$

Power is the rate of doing work ($F \times D$). It consists of strength (force) and speed (D/t). Power depends on strength and speed and the energy to sustain intense contractions.

Anaerobic Power

Chapter 2 discussed anaerobic energy sources, including ATP and CP as well as muscle glycogen. Anaerobic training leads to increased supplies of nonoxidative energy sources (ATP and CP) and improves enzyme activity in the pathway that extracts energy from glycogen in the absence of oxygen (glycolysis). Thus, the proper training will increase a skier's ability to sustain bursts of anaerobic power.

Strength

The force output of a muscle is proportional to its cross-sectional area. Strength training improves force when it leads to increased contractile protein, actin and myosin, and tougher connective tissue. Recent research has shown that strength training also leads to improved stores of ATP, CP, and glycogen. So strength training can also be viewed as another form of anaerobic training.

Strength training may provide another plus for skiers. When subjects improved arm strength they were able to do 50-70% more work on a roller board without any increase in oxygen uptake (Washburn et al., 1983). In a sense, the strength training improved short-term endurance, possibly because of enhanced energy storage or increased force from each muscle fiber. As fibers gain in strength, fewer are needed to accomplish a task, allowing some to rest as others work. So strength training provides more force, or the same force for a longer period. Both will contribute to success in skiing.

Of course, there is a point at which an increase in strength no longer contributes significantly to skiing. You don't need massive muscles to succeed. Strength is probably adequate when the force needed in a single contraction is below 40% of maximal strength for that muscle group. If you use 40 lbs of force in the pole plant, you need approximately 2.5 × 40 or 100 lbs in the muscles involved. This probably varies with different skiers because of body weight and because some skiers use their arms more than others. Actual on-snow data indicates poling forces in the 25-35 lb range (Figure 4.10). The point is this: A certain amount of strength contributes to power and short-term endurance. When your strength is at least 2.5 times the resistance, you are ready to move on to endurance training.

Strength training increases muscle size, and consequently, it dilutes the mitochondrial density relative to the muscle mass. This means you have fewer mitochondria and aerobic enzymes per kilo-

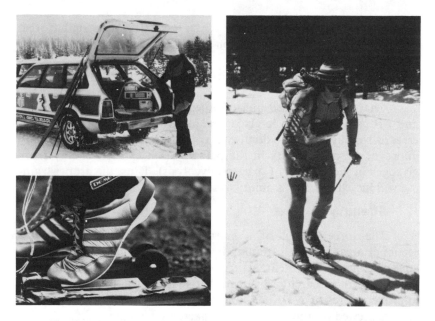

Figure 4.10 Force measurements in cross-country skiing. Measurements are taken from transducers mounted on poles and skis to determine the magnitude of force as well as how and when the force is applied. (Photographs courtesy of Dr. Charles Dillman of the US Ski Team Nordic Sportsmedicine Council.)

gram of muscle. Endurance training will restore the aerobic or oxygen-using capability you need for long-term endurance.

Speed

The velocity of fiber shortening is inherent in the muscle fiber type. Fast twitch fibers contract faster than slow fibers. We can't change fiber types so all we can do is move as fast as possible with the fibers we inherit.

Strength training improves the ability to move heavy objects at a faster rate, but it doesn't help unresisted movements much. Speed training without resistance improves the ability to move light objects, but doesn't do much for heavily resisted movements. Cross-country skiing falls somewhere in between. The goal is to move a resistance, in this case your body, as quickly as possible. Since you are moving over snow and friction is low, you don't need great force. So to improve speed in cross-country skiing, some training time should be devoted to rapid movements with moderate resistance.

Using 30-60% of maximal force and doing contractions as fast as possible will build speed, force, and power. Roller boards, Universal, Nautilus and Mini gyms, free weights, resisted calisthenics, and other methods can be used, as can plyometrics and specific skiing drills. As the season approaches, it's time to put the devices aside and do speed training on the snow, timing measured intervals while sharpening technique and neuromuscular coordination.

Power Curves. Skiers have been measured for force and power over a range of movement speeds. Dr. Chuck Dillman has shown that arms and legs work at velocities approaching 240 degrees per second during ski racing. So my colleagues and I were interested to see if skiers' power scores peaked at the limb velocities used in the sport. Figure 4.11a shows the arm and leg power curves for a top US Junior skier. Notice how his right and left scores are similar for each limb and how they peak at 240 degrees per second. Figure 4.11b shows another fine skier with dissimilar values for right and left limbs, and a peak power below 240 degrees per second. The first skier likes to use weight machines for muscular fitness training. That probably explains the balanced right and left limb scores. He follows the power training prescription (30-60% of maximum force as *fast* as possible) and stresses tempo in roller ski and ski workouts; thus, his power is well matched to the velocities used in the sport. The second athlete could use more power training to raise power output, reduce the differences between limbs and, possibly, peak at the velocity used in ski racing.

Power curves might also be used to help athletes decide what distances they are best suited for. Studies on competitive swimmers indicate that sprinters have the highest peak power, followed by middle

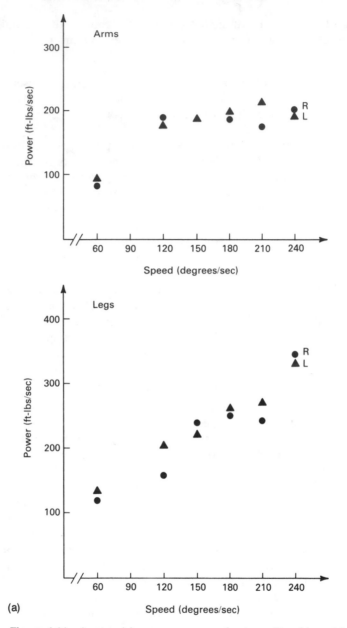

(a)

Figure 4.11 Arm and leg power curves for two elite skiers. (a) This skier's right and left power curves are similar. Both arm and leg values peak at 240 degrees/sec, the rate of contraction in ski racing. (b) This skier has dissimilar right and left power values, and all but one peak below 240 degrees/sec. Dissimilar leg values probably produce differences in stride length (stronger left leg provides more kick).

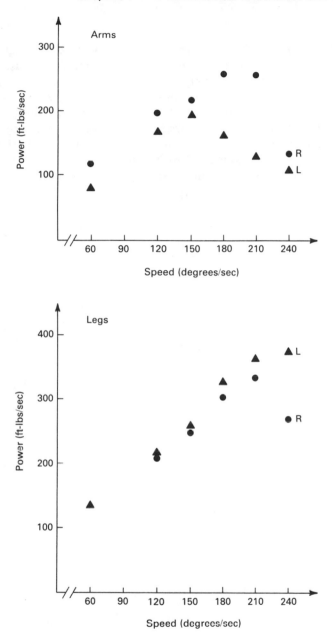

(b)

distance and distance athletes (Heusner, 1982). Those with higher percentages of slow twitch muscle fibers exert less force, peak at slower contraction velocities, and are better suited for long duration events. The same is undoubtedly true in cross-country skiing, at least at the extremes (i.e., 5 km vs. 90 km).

SUMMARY

Power is a function of anaerobic energy stores, strength, and speed. But there are other ways to get the most force from muscle. The preload discussed in Chapter 1 will generate more power in the diagonal stride, on uphill sections, and even on step turns. And remember, each of us has strengths and limitations. Skiers who are low on fast twitch fibers and speed can improve with training. However, it's best to consider your strengths and adopt a style that best suits your genetic endowment. Learn to ski your own race at your own pace and tempo instead of squandering your power and endurance in an attempt to copy another's style.

II

TRAINING GUIDELINES

It is no secret that training for cross-country ski racing is demanding work. No sport presents a greater physical or phychological challenge. Properly done, the training leads to impressive developments, but improper or overzealous training can result in injury or illness.

Training that suits the elite athlete would be destructive for the citizen racer. Similarly, the amount and intensity of training must be adjusted to suit each skier's stage of growth and development. Many factors govern a skier's rate of development, including age, heredity, experience, and physical and emotional health.

Chronological age doesn't necessarily represent an athlete's physiological development. Each child or young adult is a unique case. Physical, mental, and emotional capabilities develop at different rates in different athletes, and training that suits one may be too hard for another. So you and your coach need to take the long view and do what is best for you today *and* tomorrow, to consider the career and not just immediate, fleeting success. Both you and the sport are better served by enthusiasm and life-long involvement.

Principles
of Training

Training is a gradual process in which day-to-day changes are too small to notice. But after weeks, months, or years the transformation can be astounding. Aerobic endurance improves at the rate of 1 to 2% per week, while strength goes up 1 to 3% weekly. Both will plateau without increasing amounts of time and effort. Unfortunately, endurance declines three times faster than it is gained. So the substantial gains of training can be temporarily lost when training is interrupted by illness or injury.

This chapter will help you:

- Determine how training works;
- Appreciate the influence of individual differences;
- Develop the patience you need to gain success as an athlete or coach;
- Understand the risks of overtraining.

ADAPTATION

The regular stress of training coaxes subtle changes from the body as it adapts to the added demands imposed by training. These adaptations include improved respiration, heart function, and circula-

Figure 5.1 Training—ergometer cycle measurement of max O_2 uptake. This model of test cycle has a mini-computer and pulse measurement.

tion; increased muscle strength, endurance, and power; stronger bones, tendons, ligaments, and connective tissue. Training is a slow process. Sports scientist Ned Fredrick (1973) calls it a "gentle pastime" that cannot be rushed. Candidates for illness or injury are those who push too hard or too fast.

OVERLOAD

For improvement to take place, training must impose a demand on the body systems. More load should be added as the body adapts to the increasing workload. Improvement is related to the frequency, intensity (load), and time (duration) of the training. The overload stimulates changes in the muscles and other systems. Strength overload increases the muscle protein involved in contractions, and endurance overload leads to improvements in the muscle's ability to use oxygen.

SPECIFICITY

The type of training you do must relate to the desired results, for specific training brings specific results. Because performance improves when training is specific to the activity, heavy weight training, cycling, or swimming aren't the best ways to prepare for skiing. Recent research confirms this principle in many ways. All aspects of training have specific consequences: Distance, tempo, speed, and resistance all lead to specific results in the organs and systems used, in specific muscle fibers and fiber types (fast and slow twitch), and in specific metabolic pathways and energy sources.

For skiers, this principle means ski, ski, ski. When the snow is gone, the next best thing is the most specific substitute available. Cycling or running will provide variety and load leg muscles, but excellence in skiing requires a lot of roller skiing, ski striding, and related activities. As one respected ski coach has said, "Don't go out the door without your poles."

Of course, every rule has its exception and any principle can be carried to the extreme. As discussed in Chapter 10, weight training has its place, as do running, cycling, and other activities. The key is to use them wisely, never losing sight of the goal: excellence in cross-country skiing.

PROGRESSION

To achieve results via the overload principle, training must follow the principle of progression. When the training load is increased too quickly, the body cannot adapt, and instead, it breaks down. Slow, steady progression must be observed in terms of: *frequency*—sessions per week, per month, per year; *intensity*—training load per week, month, year; *time*—duration of training, hours (or kilometers) per week, month, year. Impatient individuals try to progress too quickly. At best they peak too early and fold; at worst they suffer injury or illness.

Progression need not imply an unrelenting increase. For example, instead of increasing weekly training distance from 40-50-60-70 km/wk, most athletes adapt better to 40-45-50-45-50-55-50-55-60 km/wk scheme. It takes a bit longer, but it is a lot easier to take.

REGRESSION

Most of the adaptations achieved with long hours of hard training are reversible. It takes three times as long to gain endurance as it does to lose it. With complete bed rest, aerobic fitness declines at the rate of 9% per week. Strength is lost at a slower rate, but lack of use will weaken even the best trained muscles. This explains why overtraining is such a risk. It leads to illness or injury, and both put a halt to training.

This principle also explains why off-season training programs are so important. Long layoffs allow hard-won training gains to regress, to go back to a lower level. The smart athlete builds on each season's gains and progresses to a higher level of performance.

LONG-TERM TRAINING

The changes that result from the progressive overload of body systems lead to impressive improvements in performance. However, it takes months and years of dedication and effort to approach excellence. This long-term training allows for:

- Gradual physiological development,
- Growth and maturation,
- Refinement of skills,
- Learning of strategy, and
- A greater understanding of the sport.

Prolonged training implies specialization. Those who hope to reach their potential concentrate on one sport. Some world-class cross-country skiers log 10,000 kilometers of training annually. That volume of training can only be achieved by mature athletes who have trained for years to develop a solid foundation, gradually increasing

Figure 5.2 Leg press apparatus, used in Sequence Exercise training which is now being used by top National Team racers in Scandinavia.

the quantity and quality of skiing, roller skiing, and other training activities. Excellence comes to those who pursue it in a well-planned, long-term training program.

WARM-UP

A good warm-up must always precede strenuous activity. This is because warming up increases body and muscle temperature as well as respiration and blood flow; it also reduces soreness and guards against muscle, tendon, and ligament strains and tears.

Warming up makes muscles more efficient, for it improves oxygen supply and helps conserve the energy needed later in the race. Static stretching, calisthenics, and easy skiing all provide a good warm-up. After this, you should concentrate on good form for several minutes of brisk skiing. Warming up is necessary before every workout, time trial, and race.

COOL-DOWN

Believe it or not, even skiers must cool down. It's possible to cool down too fast after a ski race; several racers flirted with life-threatening hypothermia in a recent ski marathon. Year-round training can make the cool-down even more necessary on warm summer days.

Complete rest after vigorous activity allows blood to pool in the veins, slowing the removal of waste products from hard-worked muscles and leading to stiffness or cramps. The light activity of a cool-down continues the pumping action of muscles on the veins, maintaining circulation to the muscles and hastening recovery. Slow to an easy pace in the last kilometer of the workout, then do some stretching of stiff or sore muscles before hitting the shower, sauna, or hot tub.

Cooling down too quickly after a hard effort results in rapid evaporation of sweat, which can quickly chill the body. Combined with fatigue and depleted energy supplies, the rapidly cooled body has little resistance to infection or hypothermia. It's important to cover up, dry off, and keep warm. And to avoid stiffness, don't cram your tired body into a small car for a long ride until you have recovered from the effort.

VARIATION

To avoid boredom and staleness as well as the more serious consequences of overtraining—illness and injury—the training program must be varied. Included in this principle are the concepts: work/rest—hard/easy.

Work/Rest

The body thrives on activity, but it does need rest. Rest and recuperation are needed after long training sessions, after hard weeks and demanding periods of the season. Adequate rest is crucial because it gives the body time to adapt, allows microscopic tears and injuries to recover, and enables fatigue by-products to be removed and metabolized. Failure to rest adequately can nullify the effects of training.

If you don't allow your body to rest to make the adaptations brought on by training, the beneficial changes will not take place. The need for rest is an individual affair, determined by each individual's level of fitness, nutrition, state of maturity, and other factors. Less fit athletes recover and adapt to training at a slower rate. As fitness improves, less rest is needed between training sessions. Highly trained athletes train two or even three times per day, but each session isn't harder than the last.

Hard/Easy

The volume of training required to achieve success in cross-country skiing would be impossible if each workout was harder than the last. The conflicting requirements of overload, progression, and rest are accomplished with the hard/easy approach. Follow a hard workout with an easy one (or a day off), a fast workout with a slower one, a long workout with a shorter one, a dull workout with an enjoyable one (e.g., playing games, working on turns, having relays).

Those who follow the hard/easy approach will be less likely to become overtired or bored. It is better to give up a day of training than to risk becoming stale or run-down. Smart coaches and athletes know that some competitions should be taken lightly. Early season races can be viewed as part of the training program or as a chance to work on pace or form. When training or competition become too demanding or boring, it's important to do something different. Variety can diminish monotony and lighten the physical and psychological demands of serious training. The only risk of the hard/easy concept is the possibility of peaking a few days later in the season. However, disregarding the hard/easy and work/rest concepts may eliminate the possibility of peaking altogether.

MODERATION

This principle lends itself to every aspect of life. Dedication is fine as long as it is tempered by judgment and moderation. Too much of anything can be bad for your physical and psychological health. Training too hard, too fast, or too long will cause the body to deteriorate. Practice moderation in all things. Don't sacrifice the future to achieve immediate success. Remember this:

> Fame, if you win it,
> Comes and goes in a minute. . . .

Approach training with moderation, knowing that overtraining is far more disastrous than undertraining. More often than not, success comes to those who pace themselves. Some may burn brightly and then fade; others are in the race until the end, practicing self-discipline, judgment, moderation.

INDIVIDUAL DIFFERENCES

Individuals respond somewhat differently to the same training. The reasons may be due to one or more of the following:

- Heredity,
- Maturity,
- Nutrition,
- Rest and sleep,
- Level of fitness, and
- Disease or injury.

Each athlete inherits more or less potential. Each grows and develops at a different rate. Growth spurts help some achieve early success, but with time, the differences tend to average out. Accept your own abilities and limits and make the best of what you've got.

POTENTIAL

Each of us inherits a potential maximal level of performance, but most of us never come close to that potential. This means that your best performances are still to be achieved. However, no one can ever achieve that potential as an athlete or a human being without dedication to a long-term program of self-improvement by setting reasonable training and performance goals and working toward those goals. New goals should take the place of old ones, those you've already obtained. Each goal you meet gives you the confidence to set higher ones, to raise your level of aspiration, to move ever closer to that elusive but achievable goal. And what better way to spend your life than in search for the best that's in you—your potential.

Figure 5.3   Sprint race, 1981 Birkebeiner week, Telemark, Cable, Wisconsin.

SUMMARY

Athletes and coaches should understand and practice the principles of training. They don't need to be experts in physiology, but they do need to listen to and heed the signals coming from the skier's body. The consequences of overtraining range from boredom and staleness to illness and injury. Even worse is the risk that a skier will push too hard, burn out, and drop out from competitive skiing. Follow the principles of training and you will avoid these pitfalls.

The Stages
of Skiing

Most kids can walk well by 12 to 14 months, and pedal a tricycle within 36 months. But it takes 4 to 5 years before they develop one-foot balance and the heel-to-toe walk. Although this doesn't mean some children can't learn to ski at an early age, it does mean you shouldn't expect too much from them.

This chapter will help you:

- Understand the stages of growth and development;
- Appreciate the importance of adjusting training programs to fit the stages;
- Determine training goals for athletes in each stage of skiing.

GROWTH AND DEVELOPMENT

Early Childhood

During years 2 to 6, the nervous and muscular systems are maturing. This is a period of rapid growth and development, a fine time to develop the basic movements that will later be used in skiing. In fact, some experts believe that this is a crucial time for motor skills development, and that children denied such experiences at this stage may have trouble acquiring complex skills later in life. Skills such as

Figure 6.1   Children line up before start of annual Holmenkollen children's ski day, held in 1982 as part of World Ski Championships.

skiing can be acquired by many children when they are given the opportunity. In countries where skiing is a way of life, the early introduction is usually gradual and natural. Children should not be forced into any sport during this period.

Late Childhood

Years 6 to 12 mark the late childhood stage. Early in this period nerve fibers become completely insulated, allowing more effective muscle control. Skills learned earlier can be refined, and while muscle strength improves it is still too early for serious physical training. Strength and endurance can be improved in this preadolescent period but no child should ever overtrain.* More substantial gains will be possible after the onset of puberty. This time is one of slow, steady growth.

Adolescence

Starting at around 12 to 14 years of age and marked by the onset of puberty, adolescence signals a period of rapid growth and matura-

*While it is too early for kids to use weights, they can engage in calisthenic-type exercises, using their own body weight to build strength and endurance.

tion. Secondary sex characteristics emerge, muscles develop, and bones grow. During this period of rapid growth, coordination and balance may suffer as muscle development lags behind long bone growth. This temporary situation fades with an adequate mixture of exercise, rest, and good nutrition. Early-maturing athletes may surge ahead in practice and competition, only to be caught and eventually passed. This and other problems of adolescence make it an interesting age to coach.

Bone growth takes place at growth plates (epiphyseal plates) located near each end of long bones like the femur (thigh bone). These growth areas are less dense than fully formed bone and more suscepti-ble to injury. As youthful growth terminates, the plates fuse with the shaft and the growth region disappears. This occurs at 19 to 21 years and signals the end of the adolescent period.

Training during adolescence, if not overdone, leads to im-provements that cannot be achieved later in life. Endurance training can improve oxygen uptake 33% or more. Cardiac muscle and heart size may undergo physiological adaptations that cannot be achieved later. Strength training between years 14 and 21 seems to provide the optimal stimulus for the development of muscle force and power.

Of course, too much training during a period of rapid growth and development can rob muscles and organs of the energy and nutrients they need. That is why there must be a careful balance between work and rest, and why these young athletes must eat a balanced and nutritious diet (see Chapter 11).

Young Adult

This stage offers athletes their finest hour. From the age of 21 to the late 30s, young adults enjoy their peak periods for aerobic en-durance and muscular power. Combined with the psychological maturity to practice hard and compete intelligently, it leads to per-sonal records and consistent performances.

This isn't an easy time for athletes, however. Society expects them to devote the time and effort to succeed in their sport and to pur-sue a career and establish a family at the same time. Small wonder many fine athletes fail to achieve their potential, as they are torn be-tween their sport and college, career, and family. There need to be ways to help athletes train *while* they complete studies, establish careers, and start families.

Mature Adult

Physiological capabilities decline with age, but not as fast as you might expect. Aerobic fitness declines less than 4% per decade for those who remain active, and strength doesn't diminish significantly until well after 55 years of age. But power, especially anaerobic power, drops more rapidly.

Happily, one thing that doesn't wither with age is the desire to participate and challenge oneself, to train and reach reasonable goals. Cross-country skiing offers such opportunities, to train year-round in a sport that offers variety without nagging injury, to develop the entire body, to compete in a challenge of skill and determination, against your contemporaries, the elements, and the clock.

STAGES OF SKIING

Just as there are stages of development, so too are there stages of skiing. Just as physical factors change with age, so do social and emotional ones. The elite national competitor has different needs and goals in sport than does the 12-year-old kid in his or her first big race. They may both wear stretch suits and a racing bib, but it would be wrong to assume they share the same motivation and drive. The stages of skiing take into consideration the different physical, social, and emotional phases of growth and development.

Kids (6-10 Years)

This is the period to awaken an interest and love for cross-country skiing. Emphasis in this period should be on learning basic skills, but it is equally if not more important that the kids have fun in the process. Kids learn best by imitation; they need good models to follow, short work sessions, and lots of games to play. Races, when they are held, should be in the form of relays to minimize the large individual differences in growth and development.

Youth (11-15 Years)

At this stage boys and girls are able to learn a variety of skiing skills and should pay more attention to proper technique. These kids are going into puberty, so it is too early to increase training dramatically, but soon enough to lay the foundation for more quality and quantity in training. There shouldn't be too much emphasis on success in races at this stage. Early developers achieve early success, only to be disappointed as others catch up or pass them.

Cooperation and performance should take precedence over competition; our society places sufficient emphasis on competition. Skiers cooperate when they train together, when they share information, waxing secrets, and feelings. Young athletes should strive for good performances, not just winning. Potential champions may get discouraged and quit if winning is the only goal. Performers gain satisfaction when they ski well; competitors are only satisfied when they win.

Figure 6.2 Holmenkollen, where the annual Holmenkollen Games have been held for over 100 years.

Young Adult (16-19 Years)

By this time, most (but not all) skiers are ready to make substantial increases in the amount and type of training. Year-round programs utilize specific training to prepare muscles for skiing. Training volume is increased and, when possible, the amount of on-snow training is expanded.

By now many skiers are strong enough for long sessions, twice daily training and intervals. However, skiers caught up in a growth spurt may need less training and more rest. As stated earlier, chronological age is a poor indicator of physiological development. No tired adolescent should be pushed toward illness or overuse injuries just to achieve short-term success.

Adult (20-39 Years)

These years can bring athletes their top performances. Technique and efficiency are at their peak, as are the physiological capabilities of endurance, strength, and power. It takes years to achieve this union of technique and capacity, and once achieved it can be maintained longer than most athletes imagine. Most leave the sport, not because they cannot keep up, but because the demands of job and family interfere with training.

Mature athletes need support, not a drill sergeant. They need opportunity, not a pep talk. Most mature athletes are highly motivated. They need the opportunity to train under the guidance of a knowledgeable coach. They need a school or job that recognizes the need for long hours of training. They need family members who understand their dedication and share their goals. Given this support adult athletes can compete into their late 30s—and beyond.

Mature Adult (40 and Over)

Training and competition don't stop when college, regional, or national team membership ends. The years beyond hold excitement and satisfaction for senior skiers. Citizen races, ski marathons, club races, even helping as a coach, race organizer, or ski club official can occupy your time and enrich your life. This may be the most satisfying stage of all, where you can begin to pay your debts by helping others as you were once helped.

Figure 6.3 Training on roller skis.

Organize a ski club to help introduce kids to the sport. Local clubs provide the framework for lifelong involvement in skiing. They teach young kids and provide the first racing experience, provide programs and coaching as the kids grow up, and keep them involved in citizen races with classifications and distances for all ages. Ski clubs are the base upon which a strong national program is built. Aside from a few schools and colleges with shaky budgets, the clubs provide the only ski programs with qualified coaches.

The US Ski Coaches Association has a coaching certification program that prepares skiers to become qualified coaches. Level 1 coaches are qualified to direct youth programs. Level 2 candidates combine experience with a week of study and practice to achieve the competence needed to direct club and school programs. Level 3 coaches are qualified to direct college and regional programs and become associated with the national team. Significant experience and successful completion of courses in physiology of exercise, sport psychology, and others are required to achieve Level 3 certification. Contact the US Ski Coaches Association for more information.

SUMMARY

The stages of skiing correspond to stages of physical growth and development, but athletes have different motives for participation at different stages as well. Young kids want to be part of a group, to be liked. As athletes mature they want to be respected for their accomplishments. The desire to win becomes stronger with age, and young kids shouldn't be expected to feel the way older ones do. Later in their career athletes may become performers, motivated by the desire to seek their potential. They become interested in the quality of the performance, not just winning. This is the sort of motivation that keeps athletes involved into their 30s, that maintains interest in the over-40 set . . . and beyond.

Training load and emotional climate must be adjusted to meet the needs and abilities of each athlete. Both coaches and athletes must be sensitive to the individual differences that exist between and within age groups. Let's face it, there aren't that many cross-country ski racers; we can't afford to lose a single one.

The Training Prescription

Training is a potent agent that coaxes specific responses from the body. As with other treatments or drugs, the dosage must be prescribed carefully to obtain its benefits and prevent any harmful side effects. Just the right amount of training leads to the desired results; too little and the changes won't take place, too much and you may undo previous progress.

This chapter will help you:

- Identify the factors involved in the training prescription;
- Learn how to use your heart rate to control training intensity;
- Establish training guidelines according to age and level of fitness.

Training programs are designed to bring about improvements in specific energy supplies, energy pathways, and muscle fibers. The intensity of training must be adjusted to meet training goals, so a training prescription tells you how hard you need to train.

Your exercise heart rate is the best guide to training intensity for the following reasons:

- It is directly related to oxygen intake and cardiac ouput.

- It increases as you move from aerobic to anaerobic effort.
- It goes up with tempo and the recruitment of fast twitch muscle fibers.
- Its increase means you are gradually switching from fat to carbohydrate for energy.

Knowing how to take a heart or pulse rate essentially means you can personalize and control the intensity of the training program.

HEART RATE

The heart rate is controlled by the cardiac control center in the brain, which receives information from the body and speeds up or slows down the heart to meet the demand for oxygen and energy. As we exercise and our muscles need more oxygen, the heart rate accelerates. You can count the heart rate by placing your fingers below your left breast. A more convenient technique is to count the pulse on the radial artery at the wrist. Simply lay your right hand in your left palm face up. Then slide the fingers of your left hand down the right thumb to the wrist and find the pulse in the groove above, or up the arm from, the thumb (Figure 7.1).

Resting Heart Rate

The resting heart rate is a good guide to the state of training because the heart rate declines as fitness improves. Mine is 40 when I'm in good shape and I've seen many in the low 30s. Unfortunately, we can't use resting heart rates alone to estimate fitness; there are too

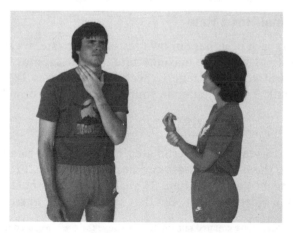

Figure 7.1   Taking the heart rate. Use the radial pulse on right at rest and the carotid on left during or just after vigorous effort.

many individual variations. But for you, the day-to-day heart rate tells you a lot about your fitness and your health.

It's best to take the resting rate frequently, in the morning before rising. You'll find it goes up when you are not feeling well or when you have a fever. Feeling ill and having a resting rate more than 5 beats above average means it's time to ease up or take a day off from training. It may mean a cold is on its way, and a day of rest could hasten your recovery.

Exercise Heart Rate

The exercise heart rate is best found by placing your fingers *lightly* along the throat just to the side of the windpipe (see Figure 7.1). The beat is particularly strong here during or just after exercise. The exercise heart rate is the best indication of exercise intensity. It is closely related to the amount of blood being pumped, the amount of oxygen being used, and the number of calories being burned. The relationship is so precise it forms a straight line that allows one to be predicted from the other (see Figure 7.2). That is why the use of the heart rate is encouraged as a guide to training intensity.

As the exercise rate goes up, it indicates a gradual switch from fat to carbohydrate as a source of energy. As it goes even higher, it coincides with a shift from aerobic or oxidative to anaerobic or nonoxidative energy production. Also, since we use slow muscle fibers for slow activity and fast fibers for faster effort, the rising exercise heart rate coincides with recruitment of the fast twitch fibers. If that all sounds a bit too complicated, don't worry; all you have to do is follow the prescription. The exercise heart rate is your proof that you are training at the correct intensity.

Maximal Heart Rate

Just as each of us has our own resting heart rate, we each have a maximal rate as well. The maximal rate is, as it says, as high as the heart rate will go.* Last time I checked mine it was 185 beats per minute (bpm). You can estimate your rate with this formula:

$$\text{Max HR} = 220 - \text{your age}$$

For a 16-year-old, the estimated maximal heart rate is 204. As you can see, the maximal heart rate declines with age. From the formula you might guess that I am 35 years old. You would be wrong, however; I'm older than that. But that raises another interesting point

*Some skiers have counted maximal rates above the rate measured in the laboratory. This seems to happen briefly after extremely hard effort combined with a high body temperature.

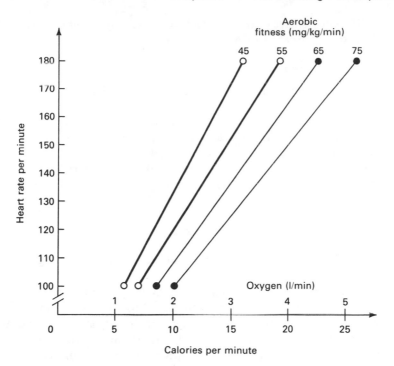

Figure 7.2   Predicting oxygen intake and calories burned during physical activity from the heart rate. Find the line that approximates your aerobic fitness. Read across from the exercise heart rate, then down to determine oxygen intake and calories burned. A skier with a 165 heart rate and a 65 (ml/kg/min) fitness score will be burning approximately 20 calories per minute (1200 per hour!). *Note.* 15-second pulse count taken immediately after exercise (15-second rate × 4 = rate/minute).

about the maximal heart rate: The rate of decline with age is slower in more active individuals. You should also know that highly-trained young endurance athletes usually average lower maximal rates than their less active friends. So, highly-trained young endurance athletes should use the following formula to calculate maximal heart rate:

$$\text{Max HR} = 210 - \text{your age}$$

Training Heart Rate

The training heart rate gauges the intensity of training. It helps answer the ever-present worries: Am I going fast enough? Am I going too fast? Using the training heart rate provided for each phase of training assures you that you are doing the right thing for your energy sources, energy pathways, and muscle fiber types.

The early stages of training call for slow, easy endurance work at an intensity of 70-85% of max HR. For example:

$$\text{Max HR} = 200 \times 70\% = 140 \text{ bpm}$$

$$\text{Max HR} = 200 \times 85\% = 170 \text{ bpm}$$

To achieve the training goals, you must train within this zone of 140-170 bpm. To be sure you are in the zone, that you are training at the right intensity, exercise at the pace you think is correct for at least 5 minutes then stop and *immediately* take your heart rate for 15 seconds. Then multiply this number by 4 to get the rate in beats per minute.

$$\text{HR} = 38 \text{ beats} \times 4 = 152 \text{ bpm} \ldots \text{right on!}$$

If the rate is too slow increase your pace a bit. If it is too high, slow down.

The training heart rate is a way of gauging the intensity of training, but remember, it is only an estimate. Those whose maximal heart rate is quite different than the average for their age may have to adjust the prescription (see Figure 7.3). So if the training heart rates seems too hard or too easy, make an adjustment. Or find your actual max HR in one of two ways:

1. Take an electrocardiogram-monitored exercise test on a treadmill or bicycle. Be sure you continue as long as you can to determine your actual max HR, or
2. Do the 1-1/2 mile run test (see Appendix A). As you enter the last quarter mile, increase your pace so you are going all out for the last 220 yards. After the run, *stop* and immediately check your rate. Just be sure you're in good condition before you attempt this approach.

Table 7.1 outlines the purpose of various training intensities.

Chapter 8 will explain the rationale behind each phase of training and how the training heart rate relates to the desired training effects. Also, Chapter 10 will demonstrate how the different aspects of training fit into a coherent training program using the principles discussed in Chapter 6.

AN ALTERNATIVE TO EXERCISE HEART RATE

If you find that heart rate checks are a bother, an alternative does exist. The body has thousands of nerves sensing pain, pressure,

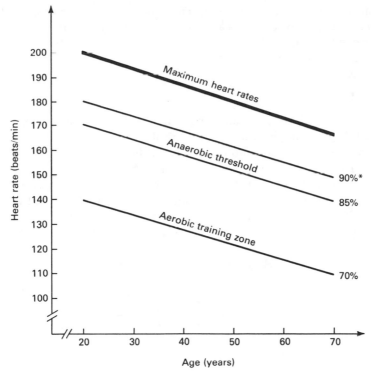

*Percent of maximal heart rate

Figure 7.3 The athlete's aerobic training zones.

TABLE 7.1   The Purpose of Various Training Intensities

% Maximum Heart Rate	Purpose
70-85	Aerobic energy sources Aerobic energy pathways Slow twitch muscle fibers
85-95	Aerobic energy pathways Recruit FOG fibers Aerobic glycolysis Oxygen transport system
95-100	Anaerobic energy pathways FG fibers Anaerobic glycolysis
100	Anaerobic energy sources Anaerobic energy pathways Fast twitch fibers Speed

temperature, and other stimuli. These nerves send messages to the brain, which then computes a composite sense or perception of effort. You can learn to read these signals and bypass the need for heart rate checks, for perceived exertion is closely related to heart rate. How does it work?

Perceived Exertion

Perceived exertion can be measured with the scale developed by Swedish psychologist Gunnar Borg (Table 7.2). Instead of taking a heart rate check, you simply ask yourself how the exercise feels.

During the early days of training use the heart rate *and* the scale. Eventually you won't need the heart rate; you'll be able to gauge exercise intensity with your own, fine-tuned sense of effort. If the training prescription calls for training at a heart rate of 150 bpm, work at the level you judge as *hard* (rating of 15) and you won't be far off.

$$\text{Hard} = 15 \times 10 = 150 \text{ bpm}$$

TABLE 7.2   Perceived Exertion

How Does the Exercise Feel?	Rating
	6
Very, very light	7
	8
Very light	9
	10
Fairly light	11
	12
Somewhat hard	13
	14
Hard	15
	16
Very hard	17
	18
Very, very hard	19
	20

Note: Rating × 10 is approximately equal to the exercise heart rate.

TRAINING CONSIDERATIONS

Several factors complicate the use of the heart rate as an indicator of training intensity. They range from emotions and illness to heat and altitude, and include the type of exercise involved. We'll consider each briefly.

Emotions

The heart rate speeds up with emotional involvement. Fear and excitement are two examples of situations in which the heart rate isn't an accurate estimate of effort. Neither of these should be a problem during practice, however.

Illness

A fever will elevate the temperature, but then you shouldn't be training with a fever. Also, after a period of bed rest, your heart rate will be unusually high, so it's necessary after illness to adjust gradually to vigorous training.

Heat

Exercise in a hot environment raises the heart rate so the body can send blood to the working muscles as well as to the skin to lose heat. Therefore, when it is unusually hot, the heart rate is not a good indicator of training intensity. Dehydration also makes the heart rate climb; obviously, however, you shouldn't be dehydrated during practice and competition. Use the prescribed HR to avoid overwork in the heat.

Altitude

During the first weeks at an altitude above 5000 feet the exercise heart rate could be somewhat elevated, but the effect usually goes away in 2 weeks.

Types of Exercise

During work with the arms alone, as in double poling, the heart rate is higher than it is for equivalent work performed by the legs (see Figure 4.1). However, the problem corrects itself when the arms and legs work together.

SUMMARY

To ensure the right dose of exercise, begin with the heart rate to guide your training intensity. But once you become familiar with the sensations of vigorous activity, you'll be able to shift from the objective, physiological prescription of training and begin to enjoy the subjective, emotional approach. You will move from the science of training to the *art*; you'll listen to your own body, not to some numbers or words in a book. When you achieve that transition, training will become safer, more enjoyable, and more effective.

The heart rate can also be used to personalize interval training workouts, thereby helping less able skiers avoid excess lactic acid ac-

Figure 7.4 Exercise heart rate. Many skiers use a heart rate monitor (top) to keep track of the heart rate during exercise. The tape recorder (middle left) and the cardiac telemetry transmitter (middle right) are used to gather research data during training or races. The quartz metronome (bottom) can be used to pace a faster skiing tempo (stride rate).

cumulation in early intervals (Figure 7.4). You can use the recovery heart rates to see if you are ready to go again. The rate should be down to 120 bpm before the next work interval. In time, you'll only need to use the heart rate occasionally, as you learn to listen to your body.

In short, you must learn to listen to and trust your feelings. You must not try to hide fatigue to please your coach or to keep up with less tired teammates. Not listening to your feelings is one of the easiest ways to put yourself out for the season. So instead of overtraining, rest an interval or knock off early.

THE TRAINING
PROGRAM

Today, neither the objective conclusions of the researchers nor the empirical observations of successful coaches point to one single proven system of training. The problems of how far, how fast, and how often to train for optimum competitive results are still not completely answered. But that doesn't mean I can't provide a program that works, a plan that is based on the experiences of outstanding coaches as well as research findings.

By working together, athletes and coches often discover training secrets that seem to work. I can't pass on these secrets, however, until I am confident they are based on a sound physiological mechanism or are substantiated by carefully conducted research. To be acceptable, the research must be based on athletes of the same age and performance level as those who will use the training method. The athlete's training log is a storehouse of information. But like other forms of clinical research data, it is based on a small sample and may be confounded by some sort of placebo or halo* effect. However, if a training technique is widely used with success, and if it is based on a physiological mechanism, it deserves your consideration.

Ultimately, you will be able to rely on judgment, experience, and intuition to decide issues and questions on training. You will develop

*If the athlete believes, it may seem to work.

personal preferences and a style of your own. Just remember to keep an open mind to new information and to listen to new research, old coaches, and veteran athletes. Adjust your thinking to keep pace with the times; almost everything research has learned about training has been reported in the last 15 years. Imagine what the next 15 will yield!

Energy Training

This chapter outlines a simple plan that ensures optimum training of the energy supplies and energy pathways used in cross-country ski racing. It will help you:

- Develop a safe and effective sequence for training energy supplies and pathways;
- Apply the principles of specificity, progression, and adaptation in your program.

The main features of the program can be illustrated in the training pyramid (Figure 8.1). The strength of the program is its strong aerobic foundation. Without this foundation, the entire program could collapse. Then comes improvement of the anaerobic threshold with more vigorous but still aerobic effort. Eventually, you will exceed the anaerobic threshold and do high intensity anaerobic training. The finishing touch to your program involves specific speed training.

A newcomer to cross-country skiing would be well advised to spend the better part of a year preparing for competition. If only a few months are available it would be foolhardy to ignore phases in the program. Be sure you spend time in each phase of training to ensure proper preparation for competition.

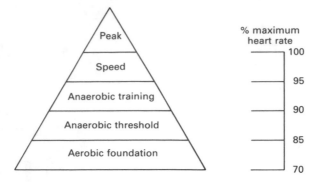

Figure 8.1 The training pyramid.

AEROBIC FOUNDATION

This phase of training is intended for the optimum development of slow twitch muscle fibers. It stimulates increases in the size and number of mitochondria, improvements in enzyme activity, and improved fat metabolism and oxygen delivery. This is the foundation upon which all future training and performance are based. Prepare well and you should find the season a success. Neglect this preparation and you will lack the stamina for more intense phases of training and competition.

Aerobic training is accomplished in long duration efforts at heart rates in the 70-85% max range. Very long sessions (over 2 hours) may be carried out at slightly lower rates. Long, slow distance training may involve the legs in running, cycling, or hiking; the arms in canoe or kayak paddling; or arms and legs in roller skiing, ski striding, rowing, swimming, or other combined activities.

Legs Alone. The ratio of running to other leg activities will depend on time, location, and individual preference. Some leg-only endurance work is needed for optimal development of the muscles, however. Combined arm and leg work limits blood flow to the legs and reduces the work load you can maintain. Leg-only exercise provides the overload to the leg muscles that will maximize improvements in energy supplies. Furthermore, changes in the muscles provide feedback to the cardiac control center, allowing a lower heart rate and a greater stroke volume due to more filling time and a greater left ventricle end diastolic volume. So, you need leg-only work to produce and maintain energy and cardiovascular changes essential to the improvement of your aerobic fitness and performance.

Arms Alone. Arm-only training, as in double poling on roller skis or paddling, is essential to the development of the combined performance. Arm aerobic development limits the combined performance until the oxygen uptake of the arms approaches 85% of the legs. Newcomers to skiing will have to spend additional time developing the aerobic fitness of their arms.

Combined. When arms and legs are combined in skiing, roller skiing, ski striding, or rowing, the oxygen transport system becomes heavily loaded. Some combined training should be included in the off season to maintain cardiovascular adjustments in heart rate, stroke volume, and cardiac output. As the season approaches, you should practice more sport-specific combined training such as ski striding, roller skiing, and, of course, snow skiing.

Training Prescription

Intensity. The keys to the development of the aerobic foundation are intensity, duration, and frequency of training. To develop it, overload the oxygen-using enzymes in slow twitch fibers with long exercise sessions, work at 70-85% of maximum heart rate to ensure significant fat utilization, increase duration and frequency to achieve progression, and extend the work periods to enhance oxygen and fat utilization. Eventually you will be able to accomplish the same effort with less carbohydrate and more fat, thereby expanding endurance and conserving muscle glycogen.

Because duration is more important at this early stage of training, you may ignore heart rate targets in longer endurance workouts. In rolling or hilly terrain, the heart rate will fluctuate with the landscape. Use the terrain to provide natural interval training but don't spend too much time in the anaerobic state. The goal at this stage of the season is the development of the aerobic foundation.

Duration. The coaches of the US Team recommend using training hours rather than kilometers or miles to keep track of training (see Table 10.1). A 17-year-old junior would aim at 400 hours of training per year; this would include skiing and running, for example, but not strength and other muscular fitness training. Training progresses from 25 hours in May (6 hrs/wk, 1 hr/day) to 30 in June (7 hrs/wk) and so forth. In August, the duration should go up to 40 hours/month (10/wk and 1.66/day on the average). That would include at least two longer sessions, with one approaching 2 hours or more. The coaches suggest that running, with and without poles, and roller skiing should make up 80% of the month's total. Of course, for those who can do it, skiing on snow is even more valuable.

Although accomplishing training goals in two or even three sessions per day is permissible, there is no substitute for continuous distance training of over 1 hour. This is especially true for skiers who race distances of 20 kilometers or more. All skiers should be sure to include at least one long workout in each week's training plan.

Frequency. Most athletes train 6 or even 7 days a week. During the off season, you can take a day off from serious training, and in fact, you may find you do better when you get the extra rest. You can spend this off day doing some activity that provides a change of pace from regular training. Hike, canoe, kayak, or play tennis on the off day, and come back to training refreshed.

As you progress in developing the aerobic foundation, you will sometimes have to train more than once a day to reach your goals. Try to vary the workouts so you won't become bored. Follow a morning run with an afternoon roller ski. When you do twice-daily training it is important to avoid excess fatigue. A training schedule should be a guide, not a slave driver. If you feel overly tired, cut back or take time off. Remember, training is a gentle pastime where you coax a series of subtle changes from the body. Don't try to rush the process.

Training Mode.

RUNNING. Begin running 20- to 30-minute sessions and increase duration to 2 hours or more. Eventually you will be ready for extended workouts on hills, with lots of natural intervals. Tim Caldwell likes occasional 4-hour workouts in the hills, using running and ski striding with poles. Dan Simoneau engages in summer road races to build his foot speed and stamina.

CYCLING. One-hour rides eventually lead to long tours, hill climbs, and races. Stand up on short, steep hills to simulate the hill climb on skis. My skiing-cycling friends look forward to their annual one-day tour from West Glacier, over Logan Pass on Glacier Park's Going-to-the-Sun Highway, down the east side, over two more passes on the way south of the park and back to the start, 145 miles and thousands of vertical feet later.

ROLLER SKIING. Begin on rolling terrain early in the summer and graduate to hill climbs. Bill Koch likes long uphill stretches followed by a ride down the mountain for safety's sake. Eventually long distance and intervals can be accomplished in good form.

SKI STRIDING. Ski striding provides another approach to combined arm and leg work and is a pleasant change of pace and location as well. It lends itself to terrain too steep for running.

Maintenance. Studies on the maintenance of aerobic fitness indicate the need for two or three endurance sessions per week. But these studies haven't evaluated the contributions of other types of training. To maintain aerobic gains, you will have to continue some aerobic training throughout the season. As training progresses to higher intensity pace and tempo work, you can't ignore the need for two or three endurance sessions each week.

Some skiers exhibit a decline in maximal oxygen uptake during the competitive season. Because the max O_2 is a rather gross test that

TABLE 8.1   Roller Skiing Guidelines

Age	Amount
Under 15 years	Introduce for short, easy efforts
15-16 years	20% roller skiing
17-18 years	30% roller skiing
18-19 years	40% roller skiing
20 and up	About 50%

may not reflect changes in the muscles used in skiing, this finding may not be important. Of greater importance is the oxidative state of skiing muscles and, of course, skiing performances.

The need for long duration workouts may depend on the distances to be skied. Long workouts are less important for a skier whose longest race is 15 km. But if you plan races of 20 km or longer, you must not ignore the need for aerobic maintenance.

Aerobic Summary

No one knows for certain the ideal amount of each type of training. It probably differs according to individual strengths and weaknesses, past experience, state of maturity, and other factors. In Table 8.1 are the US coaches' recommendations for the proportion of roller skiing during the summer months.

They feel that too much unsupervised roller skiing at an early age could lead to the formation of bad habits.* As roller skis continue to improve and become more like snow skis and as more qualified coaches become available, the use of this specific exercise could increase.

For reasons mentioned earlier, however, a fair amount of foot running and other legs-alone exercise will still be necessary to overload leg muscles adequately. Arm muscles are likely to get sufficient overload in long double pole stretches on roller skis. Remember, it is changes within the muscles that are partly responsible for the cardiovascular adjustments to training, adjustments like a lower heart rate and greater stroke volume. Total reliance on combined arm and leg exercise may allow a drop in the aerobic ability of leg muscles.

On the other hand, combined exercises overload the oxygen transport system. This training may be especially important during the developmental years (16-20) to achieve maximal development of the heart. Training that starts later in life is never as effective as that which begins before, during, or soon after puberty.

*Such as a late kick in the diagonal stride. Dr. Chuck Dillman of the US Olympic Training Center's Biomechanics Lab suggests that skiers concentrate on an early kick on roller skis.

ANAEROBIC THRESHOLD (AT)

At this stage, training should emphasize improvement of the anaerobic threshold. Faster, higher intensity efforts recruit fast oxidative glycolytic (FOG) muscle fibers, that contract more rapidly and fatigue somewhat faster than slow fibers, but do have a significant oxidative potential. If you intend to ski fast for any distance, you'll need well-trained fast oxidative glycolytic (FOG) fibers. Running, roller skiing, or skiing at the appropriate intensity stimulates aerobic adaptation in these fibers. As they improve, you should be able to work at a higher percentage of your maximum oxygen intake. Highly trained skiers on the US team average near 90%, as contrasted to untrained individuals who have anaerobic thresholds of around 50% of max.

Prescription

Training at or slightly above the anaerobic threshold maximizes the involvement of FOG fibers. If you maintain that intensity long enough to ensure aerobic metabolism, you'll initiate a training effect. Because you can't easily gauge the anaerobic threshold as a percentage of the maximal oxygen intake, I recommend the use of the heart rate as an indicator of the threshold. The 90% of max heart rate (equivalent to about 80% of max O_2) is on or slightly above the threshold for many athletes.* Since work at this intensity is difficult to sustain, interval training is the best way to start this phase of training (see Figure 8.2).

Methods.

LONG INTERVALS. Runners use 2- to 5-minute intervals to train the anaerobic threshold. Because skiing splits the workload between arms and legs, longer intervals are needed. Intervals lasting 3 to 10 minutes are appropriate on roller skis and snow skis. Start with four 3-minute intervals. The active rest interval should be at least as long as the work interval. Then, slowly increase the number of intervals (6 is plenty), increasing the length of each interval until, after 8 to 12 weeks, you are able to do four to six 10-minute intervals at 90% of the max heart rate (see Table 10.4 for interval training suggestions).

FARTLEK. Fartlek or speed play can be another form of anaerobic threshold training. This less formal approach to long intervals is best performed in natural terrain, taking advantage of hills for work and downhills for active rest. Fartlek and other forms of higher intensity training are best performed in small, well-matched groups. Skiers should take turns leading the speed play, making sure to recover adequately between bouts in order to avoid excess fatigue.

*Highly trained athletes will use 90-95% of the max HR to train the anaerobic threshold.

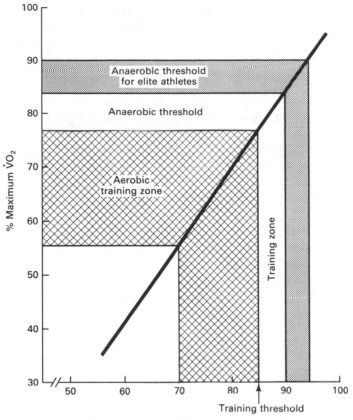

Figure 8.2 Training zones. This graph shows the relationship between percent maximal oxygen intake and the percent maximal heart rate. It outlines training zones for aerobic and anaerobic threshold training. Note that elite athletes have anaerobic thresholds approaching 90% of the maximal $\dot{V}O_2$, which corresponds to a 95% maximal heart rate.

AEROBIC INTERVALS. Aerobic intervals, another diversion from a straight interval approach, consists of numerous (30 or more) 15-20 sec pick-ups during a long, continuous effort. FOG fibers are used during the pick-ups; aerobic pathways are able to handle energy needs because they are short. Each pick-up should exceed the AT and recovery should take place below the threshold. Never start another pick-up until you feel somewhat recovered from the last.

PACE TRAINING. This involves maintaining pace and tempo for intervals of 10 to 30 minutes. Some like to do it on a measured course, others prefer to pace train in different locations so they don't become too excited or depressed with the results. You should return to the same course now and then to gauge your progress and motivate yourself. Hold race pace or slightly faster for the length of the interval, then ski easy to recover. The major difference between pace training and long intervals is the length of the work interval and the emphasis on the maintenance of pace throughout the interval. Set a standard course that is about two-thirds of the usual race distance and do it at least twice a month for time. As your anaerobic threshold goes up, your times will come down. Set modest training goals and "make haste slowly."

FAST DISTANCE. Eventually you will be able to work on or just below the AT for longer periods. Pace work and time trials are examples of fast distance training. Off-season foot races or roller ski competitions can provide the motivation you need for extended efforts.

RECOVERY. Active recovery such as easy running or skiing is used between intervals. Efforts under 10 minutes should have recovery periods at least as long as the work. Another approach to determine recovery length is to check your heart rate before beginning the next interval. The recovery rate should be down near 120 bpm before starting the next repeat. Working near the AT produces about 4 mmoles of lactic acid; unless you recover sufficiently, the lactate will still be in the muscle. Lactic acid buildup will shorten the length and quality of the session and could affect the next day's performance as well. Active recovery speeds the removal of lactic acid.

An Alternative. You don't have to continue heart rate checks to monitor training and recovery. Once you have learned what it feels like, you can approach the AT by judging such factors as respiration and perceived exertion. The rate and depth of respiration increase dramatically when you step across the AT. When you sense this disproportional increase, called breakaway ventilation, you can be reasonably sure you are at the right intensity. To be sure, occasionally check your heart rate right after an interval and use that information to adjust your sense of effort. And remember, the heart rate rises with body temperature, so respiration may be a more reliable indicator of effort intensity after a number of intervals on a hot day.

ANAEROBIC TRAINING

Training above the anaerobic threshold improves the muscles' supplies of ATP and CP and enhances the ability of the glycolytic pathway to produce ATP anaerobically. This type of training involves the fast twitch fibers, especially those fast glycolytic (FG) ones that are poorly suited for aerobic work. Cross-country skiers need this training for starts, hills, surges, and finishes. In races that are sometimes won by one 100th of a second, a racer needs every possible advantage.

Prescription

The prescription is relatively simple: work at a high intensity (i.e., 95% of max HR) for a short duration, take an active rest, and start up again. The primary method of anaerobic training is interval training, but other approaches can also be used.

Medium Intervals. Work intervals lasting 1 to 2 minutes overload the capacity of the glycolysis pathway and lead to improvements in enzyme activity. Eight to 12 repeats with an active rest interval that is twice as long as the work makes for a hard session. Young skiers should use these intervals sparingly. And because the system can only be improved a small amount, don't waste many months on anaerobic intervals. Most skiers and coaches find that 6 to 8 weeks of high intensity work is sufficient. Two to three tough sessions weekly are enough for even the most mature athletes. And be sure to count time trials or early races as tough sessions.

Short Intervals. These are 30- to 60-second efforts designed to tax the high energy supplies in the muscle, that is, ATP and CP. Do 15 to 20 at 95% of full speed using a 1:3 work/rest ratio. In cross-country these are best done up hills, and they lend themselves well to hill running and even herringbone. You can ski as far as possible up a steep grade, then run or herringbone to the top. You should make the necessary transition to diagonal or downhill before relaxing and returning for the next repeat.

Other Methods. High intensity (95% max HR) training occurs in other types of activity, such as time trials, early season races, faster-shorter natural intervals, and so on. It occurs whenever an athlete pushes well above the anaerobic threshold. Because this type of training is tiring and likely to wear some down, it should not be done too early, too often, or too hard. Sports medicine specialists in some countries go to great lengths to measure lactic acid buildup and avoid excess anaerobic training. They know that this high intensity training is more likely to lead to the overtraining syndrome characterized by staleness, illness, or overuse injury. Smart athletes will not do too many anaerobic sessions and will be careful not to push themselves too hard.

Of course, I'm not saying that you should avoid all anaerobic effort until a few weeks before the season. Some anaerobic training is acceptable throughout the year. Throw some in at the end of a run, attack a hill, do fartlek. The point is that you shouldn't attempt to raise your anaerobic capacity to its maximum months before the season and then try to keep it there. Raise it for summer running, cycling, or roller ski races if you like, then back off until the ski season. How this training fits into the peaking plan will be discussed in Chapter 10.

SPEED

Although speed training will help top off muscular energy stores, its primary value is for neuromuscular training. Fast skiing is used to fine tune the neuromuscular apparatus, to sharpen coordination, and to reset perceptual limits. It teaches you how to ski fast with efficiency, shows you how fast you can ski, and thereby makes race pace more tolerable.

Use over 20 repetitions of 15- to 45-second sprints that are 100-300 meters long. Time each effort and experiment with ways of going faster with less effort. You should terminate this and other interval work when you begin to lose good form. You can work one technique (e.g., diagonal, skate, or double pole/single kick) or choose terrain that involves a transition. Select sprints from the following:

- Starts—as in relays and races.
- Acceleration sprints—the safest way to sprint is to build up to full speed, hold, and taper.

TABLE 8.2   Effects of Training on Energy Systems

Energy System	Fiber Type	Cellular Changes	Other Changes	Method of Training
Aerobic	Slow oxidative (SO)	↑Aerobic enzymes ↑Mitochondria ↑Fat metabolism ↑Myoglobin	↑Respiration ↑Circulation ↑Musculo-skeletal (tendons, ligaments)	Long slow distance
	Fast oxidative glycolytic (FOG)	↑Aerobic enzymes ↑Mitochondria ↑Fat metabolism ↑Myoglobin	↑Heart (stroke volume) ↑Anaerobic threshold	Tempo* Faster distance and long (3-10 min) intervals
Anaerobic glycolysis	FOG and FG	↑Glycolytic enzymes		Short intervals
ATP and CP →	FOG and FG	↑ATP and CP		Sprints

*Race pace or slightly faster. Arrow indicates improvement.

- Hollow sprints—sprint, taper, then sprint again.
- Interval sprints—link many short sprints with easy effort for recovery.

Remember, you must maintain good form at all times to avoid developing bad habits.

SUMMARY

Although this chapter has outlined the essentials of energy training, this does not mean that other important changes aren't taking place in the muscles and other systems; they are. Energy training also enhances the factors involved in oxygen transport—the heart, the blood, and the circulation. Table 8.2 summarizes the effects of various types of training. Slower endurance training has its main effects on muscle enzyme systems, whereas faster aerobic training enhances the anaerobic threshold as well as cardiovascular function.

But skiing is more than energy and endurance, it involves power as well. Let's turn our attention to power and how it is developed.

9

Power Training

As noted earlier, skiing is a power-endurance sport that requires repetition of brief, forceful contractions. Muscles need the ability to contract quickly and forcibly, and they need the energy to repeat the contractions throughout the length of the race. Whereas training programs to achieve energy fitness were outlined in Chapter 8, this chapter describes how you can develop and maintain the muscular strength, endurance, power, and speed needed to win races.

When you complete this chapter you will be able to design systematic training programs to achieve and maintain:

- strength;
- muscular endurance;
- power;
- speed.

STRENGTH TRAINING

Skiing requires moderate strength. When further increases in strength no longer improve performance, it is time to move to another facet of training. How can you decide when strength is optimum, how much is enough? You can approach this question in several ways.

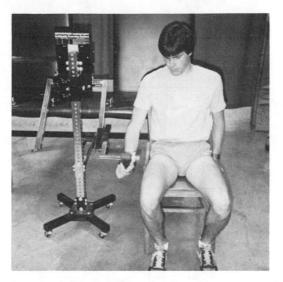

Figure 9.1 Arm and shoulder strength and power tests. An iso-kinetic test apparatus is used to determine force and power in a simulated poling maneuver.

Measurements of poling force taken on a highly skilled male skier showed 25-35 lbs of force on each pole plant. Laboratory studies suggest that contractions can be continued indefinitely when the required force is under 40% of a subject's maximum strength. This would suggest the need for strength equal to or exceeding 2.5 times the average load (e.g., 2.5 × 35 lbs = 87.5 lbs).

Strength data recorded on junior and senior male members of the US Ski Team revealed arm and shoulder poling strength ranging from 120 to 175 lbs, which would appear adequate to the task (Figure 9.1). A group of classified racers (21-31 yrs) had scores ranging from 130 to 195 lbs, proving that they too had adequate arm and shoulder strength. It also proves that strength alone won't earn you a berth on the US Ski Team.

Although poling force data is not yet available for elite female skiers, we know that women average 30 to 50% less upper body strength than males. If the average poling force is 30% less (25 lbs), then female skiers would need 2.5 × 25 or 62.5 lbs of strength in the muscle group. Upper body strength scores for women on the US Junior Team ranged from 70 to 110 lbs. The lowest value appears marginal, and this skier was encouraged to engage in an off-season strength training program. Incidentally, the coach had recognized the need for additional strength while observing the skier's technique.

A more complicated approach to the question of how much strength is enough comes from the world of work physiology. Several

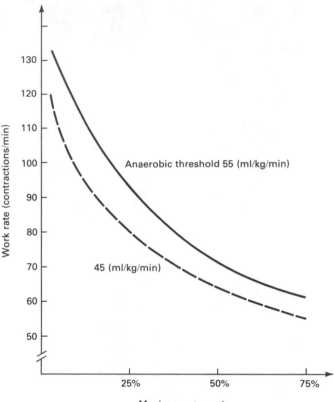

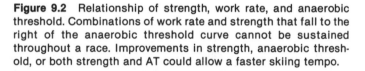

Figure 9.2 Relationship of strength, work rate, and anaerobic threshold. Combinations of work rate and strength that fall to the right of the anaerobic threshold curve cannot be sustained throughout a race. Improvements in strength, anaerobic threshold, or both strength and AT could allow a faster skiing tempo.

components of work capacity are related in a complex fashion. Shown in Figure 9.2 is the relationship between work rate, anaerobic threshold, and strength. When the combination of work rate and load (percent of max strength) fall to the right of the line representing a subject's AT, the subject cannot sustain the task throughout the race. This skier will have to either slow down or use less force with each contraction. Higher strength will allow more force, a faster rate, or more force and a faster rate. Similarly, a higher level of aerobic fitness in the arms will allow a skier to use a higher percentage of max strength, a higher tempo, or a bit more of each.

So a skier with less strength can compensate with endurance, and vice versa. The differences would be evident in technique. The skier with a high percentage of slow twitch muscle fibers and high endurance can get by with a bit less strength. And the racer with less endurance may be able to compensate by using more strength. It is difficult to generalize about the need for strength in skiing, but one thing is clear: Modern ski racing technique places more emphasis on the role of the arms, and many men and most women will profit from improved upper body strength.

The Strength Prescription

Strength improves when a muscle is placed under sufficient tension, that is, over two-thirds of max strength. It doesn't seem to matter much whether you use weights, weight machines providing constant resistance, variable resistance, accommodating resistance, or calisthenics to gain strength; they all seem to work. Some may take less time, be safer, provide a greater range of motion or resistance throughout the range of motion, but the differences among the techniques are seldom very large. What is more important is how closely you simulate the motions of skiing, both in pattern and, eventually, rate of movement. The principle of specificity suggests the need for working the muscles in the manner in which they will be employed in the sport. Thus, a modified lat pull may be more effective than the traditional, and some devices may be more specific than others.

But don't be upset if you don't have the best equipment available. Many skiers achieve national prominence using calisthenic exercises on a backyard gym. Use the equipment you have available and follow the prescription (Table 9.1).

For example, for weight training select a load that can be lifted four to six times. Train with that resistance until you can do more than eight reps, then increase the resistance. These prescriptions have been proven in a number of research studies. If improvements level off or if you want more strength, consider advanced strength training.

TABLE 9.1   Strength Training Prescriptions

Mode of Training	Repetitions	Sets	Times per Week
Isotonic (weights)	6-8 RM	3	3
Isokinetic			
Slow—over 2 sec.	8 FAP	3	3
Fast—under 1 sec.	15 FAP	3	3
Calisthenics*	6-8 RM	3	3
(Isokinetic or isotonic)			

RM = repetitions maximum, the most you can do with the weight. Increase the load when you can do more than 8 reps.
FAP = fast as possible.
Sets = a group of repetitions. Do 3 sets for *each* muscle group.
*Calisthenics such as the push-up can be used if a friend provides a resistance, or you use some other method to follow the prescription (elevate legs).

Advanced Strength Training. Serious lifters increase the training stimulus two ways: They increase sets to five or more and increase resistance (decrease reps) in some sets. This level of training takes more time. Lifters use split programs, training the upper body on a Monday-Wednesday-Friday schedule, training the trunk and legs on a Tuesday-Thursday-Saturday schedule. Training should still be three times a week for any muscle group, but the daily training should now take an hour or more. Most skiers will be able to achieve satisfactory results from the three-set, three times per week program. Of course, everyone engaged in strength training should do regular stretching exercise to maintain flexibility.

Training Guidelines. There are several guidelines for strength training, and they are listed below.

- Phase into strength training with several weeks' work with lighter weights.
- Always work with a spotter when lifting heavy weights.
- Exhale during the lift, inhale as you lower the weight.
- Alternate muscle groups during a session to allow recovery between sets.
- Keep accurate records of lifts, weights, reps, and sets.
- Test for max strength every few weeks.
- Adjust your load when you can do more than eight reps in the first of three sets.
- Maintain a balance of strength on both sides of a joint.
- Remember to warm up before every training session.
- Stretch daily to maintain flexibility.

Age and Sex. Boys and girls both benefit from strength training. Since the optimal period for strength training begins at puberty, little is gained by heavy training before that time. Prepubertal strength training may take the form of calisthenic exercises, such as chins, push-ups, and dips, where the body weight serves as the resistance.

Moderate strength training begins with adolescence and is gradually increased with maturation. Male skiers usually gain more strength and muscle size than girls due to the fact that they have considerably more testosterone, the growth-stimulating hormone. But this doesn't mean that strength training isn't just as useful for female skiers, who will eventually experience significant strength gains as well as some increase in muscle size (hypertrophy).

Progress. Strength doesn't increase rapidly, but you can expect several things to happen:

- Improvement of 1-3% per week, with the untrained muscles increasing at a faster pace;
- Faster improvement (4-5% with hard training);
- Improvements only in the muscles being trained;
- Strength plateauing as you approach your maximum potential strength.

Strength may increase 50% in 3 to 6 months; thereafter the gains come slowly and require more effort. From puberty to age 19, the improvements are more dramatic. But you can still continue to improve up to and beyond age 40.

Maintaining Strength. You can maintain strength with one maximum effort per week. Skiers must do a strength workout each week of the season to ensure that they keep their off-season training gains. Some athletes lose strength during the competitive season, so the maintenance program is necessary to ensure a high level of muscular fitness. One set of six to eight RM for each important muscle group should be sufficient.

Strength does not decline rapidly in active individuals. But inactivity caused by illness or injury leads to more rapid loss. If you must miss practice for more than a week, be sure you regain your strength and endurance before returning to strenuous competition.

MUSCULAR ENDURANCE

Cross-country skiers know the value of muscular endurance; they know how dramatically it can be improved and how rapidly it can be lost. Conventional wisdom says that exercise with less than 10 RM builds strength and that work with more than 10 RM builds endurance. Of course, building either is far more complicated than that. It is true that high resistance/low repetition exercise builds strength

TABLE 9.2   Prescriptions for Muscular Endurance

	Repetitions	Sets	Times per Week
Short-term endurance	15-25 RM	3	3
Intermediate endurance	30-50 RM	2	3
Long-term endurance*	100+	1	3

*Including numerous low resistance contractions using ski-specific movements, such as roller skiing.

and that low resistance/high repetition builds endurance (see Table 9.2). The question is, what constitutes low resistance?

Prescription

Short-term Endurance. This form of training provides a modest increase in strength along with short-term energy sources.

Intermediate Endurance. This leads to a modest increase in endurance along with some strength and short-term energy.

Long-term Endurance. This training improves the aerobic or oxygen-using abilities of the muscles, along with their ability to use fat as an energy source. After you have achieved an adequate level of strength, use sets of 25 reps on the roller board, sets of 50 or more with exergenie, apollo or mini gym, and extended double pole workouts on roller skis to develop all facets of arm and shoulder endurance. The 25 RM sets build short-term work output without improving the oxygen intake capacity, whereas high repetition training builds the aerobic enzymes needed to sustain long-term contractions. Both are needed to achieve success in cross-country ski racing.

Specificity versus Generality

Specific exercises that prepare skiing muscles are desirable, especially as the season approaches. But general exercises such as cutting and hauling firewood are useful to condition accessory muscles that may help a skier avoid injury or to back up the tiring prime movers.

Muscular Endurance Training Principles.

- Make training exercises ski specific, especially as the season approaches.
- Do as many repetitions as possible, rest, and repeat.
- Alternate muscle groups.
- Exhale on the lift as the going gets tough.
- Eat sufficient carbohydrate (rice, corn, beans, potatoes, whole grain breads and pasta) to maintain muscle energy stores.

Progress and Maintenance. Muscular endurance training has dramatic results. Repetitions can more than double in a few weeks' time. Whereas ultimate progress is dictated by one's genetic endowment and the percentage of slow and fast muscle fibers, training will improve endurance in both slow and fast fibers and substantially improve performance.

The muscle enzymes produced in endurance training are quickly lost during periods of inactivity. So once you gain muscular endurance you must work out regularly, two to three times per week, to keep what you have. So be sure to continue specific muscle endurance training up to the competitive season. Thereafter, races and training should maintain what has been gained.

The arm, shoulder, and trunk muscles are the most likely to need specific endurance training. In Appendex E are specific examples of such exercises. New skiing techniques create new training needs, and increased use of the marathon skate technique will prompt creative athletes and coaches to design new ways to develop endurance in the muscles used. Another reason to consider specific endurance exercises is to remedy weaknesses in technique. Chapter 10 will show where these training methods fit in the total program.

POWER

Power is a function of strength and speed, but it is also dependent on short-term energy sources and pathways. Power training enhances strength, speed, and energy supplies. Power can be measured in several ways. In the timed stair run (see Appendix A), an athlete runs up a flight of steps, two at a time. Power is determined by the formula:

$$\text{Power (ft/lbs/sec)} = \frac{\text{body weight} \times \text{vertical distance}}{\text{time}}$$

This measure is highly correlated with running speed for a 40- or 50-yard dash. It also tells you something about ATP and CP, the muscles' high energy stores. This test is good because it challenges muscles used in ski training and competition. (For skiing we just use the distance divided by time (D/t) since that is what counts, speed.)

Another power test is carried out on isokinetic testing apparatus such as Cybex or Orthotron. Leg power is tested with a knee extension test, which, unfortunately, does not account for the contribution of muscles that extend the foot and hip. Arm and shoulder power is tested in a simulated poling action. It is important to be able to have your power tested so you and your coach can evaluate what you're getting from your training. Unfortunately, few studies of power training have been conducted on cross-country ski racers. The prescriptions for power training are shown in Table 9.3.

Try to pattern your training after the movements of the sport; don't forget to do so in speed as well. Modern isokinetic equipment that provides variable or accommodating resistance is particularly well suited for power training, but it isn't essential.

TABLE 9.3 Prescription for Power

Resistance*	Speed	Repetitions	Sets	Times per Week
30-60%	FAP	15-25	3	3

*Percent of maximum strength
FAP = fast as possible

Plyometrics. European athletes and US skiers and jumpers have been using a calisthenic-like exercise to develop power. Called plyometrics, these explosive jumping exercises such as the Indian hop are used to improve elastic recoil and to develop power in skiing muscles. Because the body weight is about 33% of maximum leg strength, the plyos fit the power training prescription (Figure 9.3).

Do all plyo training on grass or dirt. Start gradually to avoid soreness or injury, and increase reps, sets, and the number and difficulty of exercises (see Appendix F). When you can handle three sets of several exercises, begin uphill intervals lasting 1 to 2 minutes. And when you roller ski or snow ski, attempt to translate this new-found power into improved stride length.

Plyometrics will improve strength by 8 to 10%. They will improve the muscles' ability to generate power using elastic recoil and will also increase the muscles' short-term energy stores and the ability to produce energy rapidly.

You can train for upper body power with a roller board, exergenie, apollo, mini gym, or rubber bands. Or you can use calisthenics designed for power (e.g., power dips or push-ups). For longer intervals, try double poling up a moderate grade on roller skis, emphasizing fast, forceful contractions.

Figure 9.3 Plyometrics.

You can do ski-specific power training using old skis on grassy or sandy slopes. With a little imagination, you can devise a challenging power workout. Just remember the elements of the power prescription, 15-25 reps with 30-60% of max, as fast as possible. Then develop power-endurance by extending the number of repetitions and by gradually incorporating subtle increments of power into your technique.

Progress and Maintenance. Progress is initially rapid since most athletes have never trained specifically for power. When your progress begins to plateau, you have several choices; you can do specific strength training, do specific speed training, or use more resistance in the power training prescription. For example, you could wear a weighted backpack during power training sessions.

Power associated with energy stores and enzymes is quickly lost. Therefore, you must continue a maintenance program at least once a week throughout the season. Power and strength maintenance don't require many sets so both can be accomplished in a reasonably short session. Be sure to maintain strength and power in ski-specific muscle groups and in those needed for injury prevention.

Unfortunately, as we age, power is one of the first things to go. One reason power declines before strength and endurance is that older individuals seldom do rapid, forceful contractions. Perhaps if we continue to use our power, we will be less likely to lose it as years go by.

SPEED

If any one element captures the thrill and excitement of sport it is speed. Associate US Team coach Dick Taylor calls speed an "environment" for which we need to be acclimatized, and he is right. You need to spend time in the environment to overcome fears, doubts, and apprehension. You need to become accustomed to high speed so race pace will seem, by contrast, relatively comfortable. And you need to do speed training to teach the neuromuscular apparatus how fast it can go and, perhaps, to help it go faster.

It is true that velocity of contraction is inherent in the muscle fiber, that fast twitch fibers provide more speed than slow twitch muscle. But studies have shown that the neuromuscular apparatus can be taught to do complex skills at a faster rate. The key is to practice the movements at faster than normal speeds. For example, ski down a slight grade to increase your speed and tempo in the diagonal stride. Practice rapid transitions and downhill techniques in fast but safe terrain. The point is that practice at faster-than-normal rates helps the nervous system overcome inhibitions and learn to perform at a faster tempo. The only way to perform at a fast tempo is to practice at that tempo.

Begin by spending a few minutes each day concentrating on speed. Increase this time as you adjust, but don't progress so fast that you become frustrated. Precede the speed training with enough strength and power exercises to provide the base for faster, more powerful contractions. Then, as the season approaches, integrate more specific speed work into daily practices.

Prescription

Prescriptions for speed include numerous short, all-out efforts. Specific examples may be found at the end of Chapter 8.

Speed versus Pace or Tempo. As a skier, you must understand the distinction between speed, pace, and tempo. In training, speed refers to nearly all-out effort: high speed for a short distance, to sprints. Pace refers to time over a given distance, such as 1, 5, or 10 kilometers (e.g., 3 min/km). Tempo refers to the rate of skiing or stride rate (e.g., 115 strides/min). I make the distinction so you will not be confused when your coach recommends speed or pace training. Speed training enables skiers to become familiar with the environment, to train the neuromuscular apparatus, to decrease inhibitions and, during the peaking phase, to top off the muscles' ATP and CP, the short-term, high energy supplies. Pace training on the other hand is often aerobic. It is done at the upper edge of the skier's aerobic range, at the anaerobic threshold, to increase oxygen intake, to nudge the threshold upward, and to acquaint the skier with race pace. You should experiment with tempo in both forms of training to make the most of strong points in technique and physiology.

So do speed skiing to make race pace feel easy, to reduce inhibitions, to train your nerves and muscles to move quickly, and to improve high energy stores. The small but significant increase in high energy ATP and CP may be the difference in a race timed to one 100th of a second. A well-learned skill isn't easily lost, but energy stores only remain elevated during a period of intense training. Because it takes about 6 weeks of speed training to elevate this energy, it makes sense to do your serious speed work in the weeks preceding the peak of the competitive season. Of course, some speed work throughout the other seasons of training will make you more familiar with the territory, the environment of speed.

SUMMARY

Most cross-country skiers will profit from power training, whether it be for strength, speed, or power-endurance. But improvements in power won't automatically translate into faster skiing. The improvements have to be integrated into technique, using more force

Figure 9.4 The backyard training center. See Appendix E for more ideas on a home training center.

and power to achieve a longer stride length, or using the same force at a higher tempo.

To determine what combination of force and tempo are best suited to your endowment and level of fitness, measure a 200-meter course and ski it regularly. Ski at race pace using your usual technique. Then ski with a slower or faster tempo, more or less force per kick. Time each repeat to see which combination is the fastest, and keep track of your perception of effort so you can judge which combination provides the most speed for the least effort. Of course, one of the fascinations of skiing is that conditions are always changing, so be ready to alter your style when snow, wax, skis, or fatigue dictate a change.

Finally, let me suggest a backyard training or fitness center as a convenient way to train for muscular fitness. It is always available and serves as a constant reminder of the need to develop and maintain the power and endurance required in ski racing (see Figure 9.4).

The Seasons
of Skiing

Although the snow seldom falls before November and is often gone in March, the serious ski racer trains year-round. The year-round program can be viewed as a series of seasons, each with a different flavor, each with different training goals. You soon learn to love all the seasons of skiing: the off season for its long, easy runs through the woods; the preseason for the smells of fall, the snap in the air, and the return to skiing; the early season because you're performing again; and the peak season for the thrills and excitement of the big races.

Each season is comprised of a series of cycles or periods, with each cycle lasting approximately 4 weeks. The cycling or periodization of the training load ensures moderate progression in training. Finally, training can be planned for each week of each cycle of each season.

This chapter will help you plan year-round energy and muscular fitness training programs using a systematic approach to:

- Seasonal training goals;
- Training cycles;
- Weekly plans.

PLANNING YOUR ANNUAL TRAINING PROGRAM

I can provide sensible outlines for training but it is up to you to make adjustments to suit your individual needs. Some of you will need more strength, others less; some of you will tolerate more volume, others will not. The scientific approach to training that I give you will need your insight and sensitivity, for it is the latter that constitutes the art of training.

Finally, let me say a few words about newcomers and veterans. The training program outlined in this chapter includes a gradual increase in intensity that is designed to prepare the newcomer for the demands of competition. Although veteran athletes follow the same general pattern of training, they are able to tolerate a greater training load in every season of the year. When the competitive season ends, these athletes take a week or two off, then return to training to build on the past year's gains. Because they have never really stopped training, they are capable of handling more distance, pace, and speed.

And although this program outlines a gradual preparation for the competitive season, there is no reason why a well-trained athlete can't peak in other seasons for road races, cycling, roller skiing, or rowing sports. I encourage such activity because it provides purpose, challenge, and excitement to the annual program, and because it provides racing experience and acclimatization to the environment of speed.

SEASONAL TRAINING GOALS

Skiers can divide the year into four main seasons, and each season has specific training goals (see Figure 10.1). The *off season*, ranging from a few weeks after the last race up to the end of summer, is the time to concentrate on aerobic energy training. If you need strength work, the off season is the time to give it attention. It makes sense to build muscle mass first and then develop the endurance or power capabilities. The *preseason* lasts from late summer until the first race. That is the time to concentrate on the aerobic capabilities of

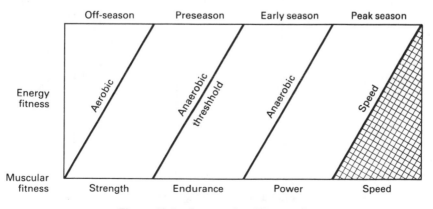

Figure 10.1 Seasonal training goals.

fast twitch muscle fibers, to raise the anaerobic threshold. Muscle endurance training logically follows strength development, and most veteran skiers will do power training as well. The *early season* includes that portion of the competitive season which serves as a preparation for more important races. This is the time to engage in anaerobic energy training and to complete the power/speed buildup for the peak season. The early season is the time to begin peaking for the important events of the season, the peak season, when your mental and physical preparation peak to allow your best performances.

While you will concentrate on certain aspects of training in certain seasons, you must also be sure to maintain the gains of the previous season. So you must remember to maintain any aerobic fitness improvements in the subsequent seasons, as well as strength and the other components of energy and muscular training. Now let's translate those goals into monthly cycles, weeks, and days of training.

Off Season

The off season consists of at least four monthly cycles or periods. Each cycle involves a progressive 3-week increase in training followed by an easier week. In practice, the fourth and easier week is roughly equivalent to the second week of the period. The next 4-week cycle starts where the last hard week ended (see Figure 10.2). Cycling or periodization provides for progression in training but also allows time for recovery.

Energy Training. Once again, the off season is the time to concentrate on aerobic training. Of course, veteran skiers should be ready

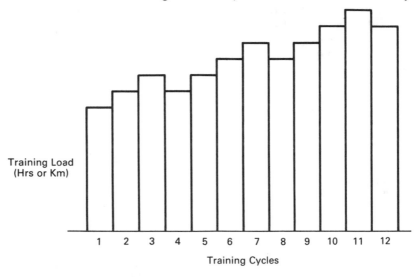

Figure 10.2 Training cycles.

and able to include other aspects of training. Unless you plan to engage in summer roller ski or other races, however, there is no reason to rush into a lot of high intensity training; you'll only burn out before the snow flies. Use the time to build the stamina you need to endure the training and competition to come. Remember, aerobic fitness is the foundation for all other training. Build a solid base so you will have the ability to recover from hard training, races, and even illness.

Table 10.1 is a guide to weekly training hours for experienced skiers as suggested by the coaches of the US Team. A newcomer should start well below the levels listed. For example, if you are a reasonably active citizen racer preparing for your first season, start off-season training with 6-7 hours per week.

TABLE 10.1   Guide to Weekly Training Hours*

Group	Hrs Yr/Hrs Wk	Off Start/End	Pre Start/End	Competitive Season
World class	800-1000/17	15/18	18/20	12-13
Elite US	500-700/12	10/13	13/16	11-12
Citizen	400-500/9	8/9	9/10	7-8
Elite junior				
17-19 yrs	500-700/12	10/13	13/15	10-11
Junior				
18 yrs	500-600/11	10/11	11/13	9-10
17 yrs	400-500/9	8/9	9/10.5	7-8
16 yrs	300-400/7	6/7	7/8.5	5.5-6.5
15 yrs	250-350/6	5/6	6/7	4.5-5.5
14 yrs	200-300/5	4.5/5.5	5.5/6.5	4-5
13 yrs	150-250/4.5	4/5	5/6	3-4

*Recommended by U.S. Ski Coaches for experienced skiers. Newcomers start 10-20% lower.

Chapter 8 provided a prescription for aerobic training, where the emphasis is on the development of the oxygen-using and fat-burning abilities of slow twitch muscle fibers. But not all energy training consists of long slow distance work. Shown in Table 10.2 is a guide to weekly training during the off season. The first column includes facets of the well-rounded program; the second column provides a menu of training modes to choose from to accomplish each aspect of training. For example, you could choose to do a long, slow distance workout on roller skis or ski running (striding or walking). You could take care of natural intervals by running or roller skiing in rolling terrain. Ideally, the pace work should be as specific to skiing as possible, so use your roller skies.

Table 10.2 also provides guidelines for times per week of each method of training and suggested training intensities (% max HR). As

TABLE 10.2   Off-season Energy Training Guide
(Build the Weekly Plan Using Both Columns)

Each Week Include	Times/ Week	HR % Max	Modes of Training	% of Total Time
Long slow distance (LSD) over 2 hrs	1	70	Roller ski Run	30-50 30-50
Hills (vertical)	1-2	80	Ski walking	
Natural intervals	1	70-85	Ski running	20-40
Fartlek	1	70-85	Ski striding	
Medium distance over 1 hr	1	80	Bicycle (standing)	10-20
Experienced athletes include			Row	
Pace	1	85-90	Paddle	
Long intervals	1	85-90	Swim	10
Speed	1	95-100	Roller skate* Other _____	

Remember, arms need aerobic training also; do extended arm workouts on roller skis and use the poles vigorously on long hill climbs (ski run, stride and walk).
*To train for skating on skis.

for modes of training, the coaches of the US Team prefer their athletes to do a high percentage of roller skiing and running. Some athletes love to bicycle, however, spending as much as three-fourths of the time standing up. Others enjoy 4 hours or more of ski striding sessions with ski poles over mountainous terrain.

Table 10.1 provides suggestions for hours of training per week in each session. Using Tables 10.1 and 10.2 an experienced 18-year-old racer could construct the following weekly plan shown in Table 10.3.

TABLE 10.3   Weekly Training Plan

Day	Type of Training	Time*	Mode
Sunday	Long, slow distance	2 hrs	Roller skiing
Monday	Natural intervals	40 min	Running
Tuesday	A.M.: Easy run	1 hr	Running
	P.M.: Pace work	30 min	Roller skiing
Wednesday	Medium distance with hills	1 hr, 40 min	Ski striding
Thursday	A.M.: Roller ski	40 min	
	P.M.: Speed work	30 min	
Friday	Fartlek	1 hr	Roller skiing
Saturday	Variety	2 hrs	Bicycling

*Total time per week: 10 hrs

In this sample, the 18-year-old did 2-a-day workouts on Tuesday and Thursday, alternated long with short, hard with easy, and used the bicycle and ski striding (running, walking) for variety.

Never forget to do aerobic training of your arms as well as your legs. The roller board, exergenie, and other training aids cannot provide the hour-long aerobic training that arms need to achieve optimal development of oxidative enzyme systems. Instead, long double-pole sessions on roller skis, and extended ski walking and striding are essential for arm endurance. Remember, poorly trained arms draw blood away from the legs but don't contribute significantly to speed in the track, thus forcing the legs to go under long before they should.

In summary, off-season energy training is designed to provide optimal development of the aerobic or oxygen-using enzyme systems of slow twitch muscle fibers. Other facets of training are included to maintain the gains of previous seasons and to prepare the body for the faster training to come.

Muscle Training. The main focus of off-season muscle training is the develoment of necessary strength. While newcomers, most women, and many junior men need additional strength, the specific level of need can be determined by an analysis of strength and/or technique. Strength improves at the rate of 1-3% per week. So you should schedule a minimum of 8 to 12 weeks for strength training. Those of you who are far below average may need even more. When strength reaches the level you desire, switch to a once-a-week maintenance program and begin endurance and/or power training. Remember, muscular fitness is developed in alternate day programs.

Why can't you train muscle strength and endurance at the same time? A study comparing strength, endurance, and simultaneous strength and endurance training had surprising results. While the strength gains of the strength/endurance group paralleled the improvement of the strength-only group for awhile, the combined group seemed unable to keep up—thus, the need to train for strength and then endurance (Hickson, 1980). Of course, this study didn't use rugged endurance athletes as subjects. But until we are certain that optimal strength gains can be achieved while doing significant endurance training with the same muscle, I'd suggest doing one then the other. Select five to six key muscle groups and follow the strength prescription (6-8 RM 3 sets, 3 × wk).

Preseason

Energy Training. In Chapter 8, the anaerobic threshold was discussed. As stated there, this stage of energy training is designed to improve the oxidative capabilities of the fast oxidative glycolytic fibers (FOG) in order to raise the anaerobic threshold. Also discussed were training methods that raise the training heart rate up to or slightly above the anaerobic threshold to recruit FOG fibers and make them work aerobically. Those methods include:

- Long intervals (3-10 min)
- Fartlek
- Aerobic intervals
- Pace training
- Fast distance

Table 10.4 is the preseason energy training guide. Use it as you did the off-season guide to build weekly training programs. Remember, you shouldn't do more than three high-intensity sessions weekly. Newcomers should begin their training with the first three methods; as the season progresses you'll be able to add pace training and fast distance work. Veterans can tolerate pace training much earlier in the season.

The 18-year-old racer described earlier in this chapter could, in the early preseason, follow the program shown as Table 10.5. You may wonder when our young skier ever gets to rest. The answer is any time she needs one. A day off now or then won't hurt, and it beats getting run down and missing an entire week. Use the overtraining index in Chapter 13 to avoid pushing yourself too hard too soon. If you follow the heart rate guidelines you should get some relief on alternate days. If you feel you need more hill work, you can work it in with natural intervals, fartlek, or even long intervals.

TABLE 10.4   Preseason Energy Training Guide

Each Week Include	Times/ Week	HR % Max	Modes of Training	% of Total Time
Long intervals	No	90-95	Roller ski	40-60
Fartlek	more	80-90	(or ski)	
Aerobic intervals	than	70-95	Run	30
Pace training	3 per	90	Ski walk	
Fast distance	week	90	Ski run	30-50
			Ski stride	
Continue to do				
Hills	1	80-85	Other	<10
Natural intervals	1	75-85		
Medium distance	1	80		
Long slow distance	1	70-75		
Speed	1	95-100		

Schedule 2-3 intensity workouts each week. Remember to train the arms in both long duration and high intensity aerobic efforts.

TABLE 10.5   Early Preseason Training Program

Day	Type of Training	Time*	Mode
Sunday	Long, slow distance	2 hr, 30 min	Roller skiing
Monday	Fartlek	1 hr	Running
Tuesday	A.M.: Medium distances over hills	1 hr	Ski striding
	P.M.: Long intervals (4 × 3 min)	40 min	Roller skiing
Wednesday	Medium distances	1 hr, 30 min	Running
Thursday	A.M.: Fartlek	1 hr	Roller skiing
	P.M.: Aerobic intervals	50 min	Running
Friday	Medium distances on hills	1 hr, 30 min	Roller skiing
Saturday	Pace training plus speed	1 hr	

*Total time: 11 hrs

Finally, be sure to include some anaerobic threshold training for the arms. When you do arm work exclusively, you cannot rely on the heart rate since the max heart rate for arms alone is often 20 beats lower. So for arm work rely on the perceived exertion rating to judge intensity (see Chapter 7). If you work at a level you judge as very hard, you should be close to the arms' anaerobic threshold. When you skate or do the single kick-double pole you can use the heart rate as your guide.

Muscle Training. At this point you should start concentrating on power-endurance, a form of training that involves rapid forceful repetitions with moderate resistance. The long-term endurance training needed for energy training comes in extended roller ski workouts and ski striding. So the muscle training can focus specifically on power-endurance. Power and short-term endurance training can be *combined* since both include similar numbers of repetitions. Do three sets of 15-25 RM as *fast as possible.* Use weight machines, plyometrics, roller boards, or calisthenics to develop power-endurance in the important muscle groups of the legs, trunk, and arms and shoulders.

LEGS. Most skiers remember to use weights or plyos to develop the muscles used in the diagonal stride. But only a few take the time to train muscles used in skating or the herringbone. You or your coach can design a weight machine and/or plyometric program to develop the quadricep and hamstring muscles of the upper leg and the calf muscles and include variations specific for skating, herringbone, and downhill skills. Start with one set of each exercise and move to two and then three sets. Do less important exercises at least twice each week and essential ones three times.

TRUNK. Soreness in the lower back during the first days of skiing or roller skiing doesn't mean your back muscles are weak. So you need only do a modest amount of back work (i.e., one set of each exercise) to ensure adequate strength and endurance. Time, stretching, warm-up, and good technique will soon get rid of your sore back.

Abdominal exercises should be done year-round. You could use the preseason to add some more demanding exercises like curlups with weights, and you could do more sets of them as well. When combined with the abdominal involvement during poling, the muscles should be in good shape by the early season.

UPPER BODY. Skiers definitely need well-trained upper bodies; the arms and shoulders need strength, endurance, and power. Pulley weights, isokinetic devices (mini gym, exergenie, or apollo), surgical tubing, inner tubes, roller board, even calisthenics, can all be used to develop power-endurance in your arms and shoulders. With devices like Nautilus or with positions like sitting or kneeling on roller board, you may be able to get a greater range of motion. Use the best equipment available and set up a program of several exercises that you will stick with during the weeks leading up to the first race.

Mode. No conclusive evidence proves that any one method of weight training or weight machine is superior to another for strength, endurance, or power. What is important is that the appropriate prescription is followed and that the exercises used be specific to the intended use. Skiing muscles are not the only ones you should train, however. In fact, there is considerable advantage in maintaining the power and endurance in muscles that may come into use when the prime movers become fatigued. So don't fret if you can't afford to work on the newest machines, or if every exercise isn't as specific as you might like. With enough roller skiing and skiing, you'll satisfy the principle of specificity (see Table 10.6).

Early Season

Contrary to what you might think, the early season is not the time to place undue emphasis on winning, unless of course you have a major race or qualifier scheduled. The early season is the time to consolidate the gains of previous training, to develop a workable race strategy, to fine tune the many skills of racing, and to begin building toward the peak of the competitive season.

Energy Training. With a strong background of aerobic and anaerobic threshold training, you should be ready for some anaerobic training. Skiing is essentially an endurance sport, but there are enough opportunities for anaerobic effort to warrant the training emphasis. The start, hills, surges, and finish sprints are all anaerobic, and train-

TABLE 10.6   Sample Preseason Muscle Training Plan*
(3 Sets of 15-25 RM—As Fast as Possible)

___

Legs—Weights or Weight Machines (optional)
  Leg press
  Partial squat or leaper
  Toe raises
  Plyometrics

___
___
___

Trunk—Back
  Back-ups
  Leg-ups

Abdomen
  Curl-ups (with weight if necessary)
  Basket hang (or pike)
  Leg lifts

Upper Body
  Weights or weight machines—modified lat pull or pullover (Nautilus)
  Roller board (kneeling, sitting or lying)
  Exergenie (apollo, mini gym)
  Other (surgical tubing, inner tube)
    (calisthenic-type such as dips, push-ups)

___

*Do 3 times per week. Increase resistance when you can do 3 sets of 25 RM.

ing should include two or three weekly sessions that push you above the anaerobic threshold and develop short-term energy stores and pathways in the fast glycolytic muscle fibers. Of course, you shouldn't abandon other aspects of training; you must still maintain your aerobic gains in the slow oxidative and fast oxidative glycolytic fibers (see Table 10.7).

With races and higher intensity training, you'll need to reduce your training volume and get more rest. Before the early season, your only goal was training. Now you'll have to perform as well, and that requires rest and recovery. Without sufficient rest, your performance will plateau. And since hard training and racing lowers the resistance, lack of rest could lead to illness.

PEAKING. Peak performances occur when the effects of training are maximal and the effects of fatigue minimal. Plan your training to peak 1 to 2 weeks before your most important races. Since it takes 6 to 8 weeks to achieve the benefits of anaerobic training, you can just count back 6 weeks from a date 1 to 2 weeks before the big races. That is when your peaking program should begin, when intensity of training increases and training volume declines, and when you need to emphasize the quality of skiing over the quantity. This period of added

TABLE 10.7   Early Season Energy Training Guide

Each Week Include	Times/ Week	HR % Max	Mode of Training	% of Total Time
Medium intervals (See Table 10.4)	2 per week*	95	Skiing	100
Short intervals		100		
Sprints (speed)		100		
Races**	1-2 per week	90	Skiing	100
Long intervals				
Pace training				
Fast distance				
(Complete the week with selections from the following)				
Long slow distance	1	75	Skiing	80-90
Natural intervals	1	75-85		
Fartlek	1	80-90	Running***	10-20
Hills	1	85		
Medium distance	1	80		

*Start with medium and short intervals.
**Followed by easy skiing and technique work on the course.
***On travel and off days to maintain aerobic capabilities of legs.

physical and emotional stress makes it especially important that you monitor the overtraining indices listed in Chapter 13.

During the early season, it is sometimes advisable to train through less important races. That means the training continues unchanged up to the day of a race and resumes soon thereafter. Although it's not the best way to win races, it does help to toughen you and prepare you for the big events to come. The early season peaking process ends 3 to 5 days before an important race of the peak season.

Keep in mind that early season race results are not the training goal, that the early season is the time to prepare for the big races, and that fatigue may sometimes mask progress. The pay-off will come when you reach your peak, taper training, and perform up to your potential.

Bill Koch ignored the newspaper reports that questioned his readiness for the 1981-82 season. He knew what his goals were in those December races. But when the World Cup series began he was ready. His World Cup victory was a testimony to careful preparation for the important races of the season. He emphasized the need to know himself, to keep good records, and to learn from his successes and failures. Koch recommends that athletes plot their peaking or performance plan. As the season progresses, you can compare your actual performance with your plan (see Figure 10.3), and when the season is over, you will see if you peaked at the right time, too soon, or too late.

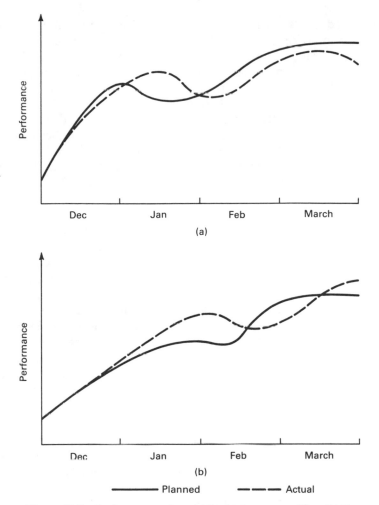

Figure 10.3 Performance plan. (a) Early season qualifier. (b) One peak plan. Adapted from Bill Koch, "Bill Koch on Training Through Racing," *Cross Country Skier*, 1981, 1, 44-46.

Muscle Training. The early season is your last chance to do serious speed training while you maintain strength, endurance, and power. Specific speed training will lead to improvements in performance by lessening the fear of going fast and by developing your neuromuscular skill. You can learn to ski faster, to tolerate faster speeds in the diagonal, single kick-double pole, double pole and skate.

SPEED TRAINING. The purpose of speed training in the early season is somewhat different than speed training for energy production, but the results probably overlap. Do a specific technique as fast as possible over a 200-meter course. Pick up your tempo and increase your speed a little each week. Move to a slight downhill grade and repeat the practice. The goal of this exercise is to become comfortable at faster speeds, tempos, and steeper grades. Your coach and fellow athletes can perform timing studies to determine what technique and tempo yield the fastest time for the terrain.

Another facet of speed training focuses on transitions—from diagonal to single kick-double pole to double pole and vice versa. Time a 10- to 20-second stretch that requires a transition; then concentrate on a facet of technique and try to do the section faster and faster. The same approach can be used for step turns and other downhill skills. Of course, you must maintain correct form throughout all the drills.

These speed drills can help you trim seconds throughout a race, and timing them will add an element of fun and competition. But be careful to choose sections that are safe; if you're in doubt, check with your coach. Don't practice on terrain that is beyond your level of ability. Work up to more challenging situations as skill and confidence grow.

Speed and tempo constitute an environment that demands acclimatization. As you spend time in the environment it becomes more familiar and more comfortable. If some of your training time is spent going faster than race pace, race pace will become more tolerable and less threatening. Many skiers go in the opposite direction; they race much faster than their practice pace, thereby growing more anxious and less confident with every stride in the race.

MAINTENANCE. You can maintain your strength with one session per week. The best time for strength maintenance is as far as possible before the next race, like Monday before a Saturday race. When possible I recommend the use of isokinetic devices, those that resist the contraction but don't require the lowering of the weight. Muscle soreness is a result of lowering the weight, as in ordinary weight training, and soreness can interfere with technique and make practice less enjoyable. Another approach is to work in pairs doing *counterforce* exercises. This approach provides resistance throughout the range of motion and can be done with two people of somewhat equal strength. One set of 8 RM should maintain strength in important muscle.

Power-endurance similarly requires one session per week for important muscle groups. One set of 15-25 RM for each important muscle group will maintain power-endurance for the racing season when accompanied with strength maintenance, speed training, and races. If January races include a lot of vertical skiing, the 3-day-a-week power-endurance program can be extended into the early season. But power contractions rapidly deplete muscle glycogen stores, so you shouldn't do a vigorous power workout within several days of a race.

Isokinetic devices, ploymetrics, and counterforce exercises can be used with the power-endurance prescription: 15-25 reps with 30-60% max, as fast as possible. You may lose some of the value of power training if you don't try to translate power into technique, so use brief, explosive contractions while you practice. During speed trials, do some repeats emphasizing explosive kicks, others concentrating on forceful leg swings or other aspects of technique. In this way, you can learn how force relates to stride length and speed. Because everyone differs in regard to optimal contraction speeds, force, and power, the practice will help each of you determine an individual, optimal level of effort and tempo.

Peak Season

Now you've arrived at the goal of the entire training program, the time when energy and muscular fitness as well as technique and mental preparation need to be at their peak. If all has gone well in training, and if you have avoided serious illness and injury, you should be ready to produce your best performances, to work up to your potential. The training goals for the rest of the season are to get lots of rest, remain healthy, and maintain the peak.

Energy Training. The guide to weekly training hours (see Table 10.2) calls for a decline in volume during the competitive seasons. After Saturday and Sunday races, the week could include the program shown in Table 10.8. A speed or tempo session on Monday or Wednesday would round out the program for the week. The length of the long, slow distance workout depends on the age of each skier. Those preparing for races of 30 and 50 kilometers should schedule a session that approaches the length of the race, at least in time. There is no substitute for extended workouts when you are preparing for longer races.

If races fall mid-week, schedule a light workout the day before. And if any phase of this maintenance training begins to wear on you, stop and rest. At this point, it is too late to force the training or correct previous training mistakes; rest and recuperation are more important.

TABLE 10.8   Energy Training Program

Day	Type of Training
Monday	Light day of easy skiing or running
Tuesday	Intervals or pace work
Wednesday	Long slow distance
Thursday	Natural intervals with hills
Friday	Easy skiing or rest
Saturday	Race or pace training
Sunday	Race or pace training

TABLE 10.9   Interval Training Guidelines

Intervals	Train	Repetitions	Duration	Work/Rest Ratio*	HR % Max
Long	Anaerobic threshold	4-6	3-10 min	1:1	90-95
Medium	Glycogen pathway	8-12	1-2 min	1:2	95-100
Short	High energy	15-25	30-60 sec	1:3	100
Sprint	Speed; high energy	25 +	10-30 sec	1:3	100

*1:3 means rest is 3 times as long as the work.

Don't waste a year's training by trying to squeeze more out of yourself than your body can handle. Especially during the competitive season, check your morning pulse carefully and get a good night's sleep.

Finally, never perform more than three high-intensity workouts per week, whatever the season. If you are skiing three races each week, the rest of your training should be moderate or light. With two races you can afford a firm interval or pace workout, but avoid exhausting anaerobic intervals. The stress of races should maintain that capability for the rest of the competitive season. See Table 10.9 for interval training guidelines.

RUNNING. One reason I recommend running during the competitive season is that it provides a way to exercise on off days and travel days, when you don't have the time to get on snow. Another reason is that it maintains tendons, ligaments, and bones so the transition to dry land training will not be so hard. Yet another reason is that it ensures sufficient intensity of effort in leg muscles.

Combined arm and leg exercise splits the cardiac output and limits the intensity of leg exercise. Since well-trained muscles provide some of the important effects of training on the heart through messages sent to the cardiac control center, it may be important to keep the major muscles of the legs trained at sufficient intensity to maintain these benefits throughout the competitive season. One to 2 days of running each week should maintain the aerobic capabilities developed during the off- and preseasons.

Muscle Training. The goal for the peak season is maintenance. Maintain strength, power-endurance, and speed of important muscle groups with one session per week. If travel and race schedules make this difficult don't worry, work the session in when you can and keep to your usual routine to avoid the risk of stiffness and soreness. The night before a race is *not* the time to try out the fancy equipment in a hotel health club. Maintain muscles in the legs, trunk, and upper body. Keep records in your training log to be sure you are indeed maintaining strength or power-endurance at the preseason level. If not, you could slip in an extra set or an extra muscle training session to edge it back up. One short set of sprints will maintain your speed; races and relays will take care of the rest.

SUMMARY

You can build your seasonal plan by following the steps listed below:

1. Determine seasonal and weekly training hours.
2. Plan cycles within the season.

3. Use the energy training guides to plan the weekly schedules.
4. Schedule appropriate muscle training on a Monday-Wednesday-Friday basis.

Then, throughout the season:

5. Monitor overtraining indices and adjust training as needed.
6. Assess progress with periodic pace workouts.
7. Keep good records of energy and muscle training activities.

IV

PERFORMANCE

A properly planned and executed training program can be enjoyable and satisfying; in fact, many skiers get hooked on training. But training is done in preparation for performance and in skiing that means races. This section deals with factors that can influence performance, such as nutrition, the environment, and illness. Good, consistent performances demand careful preparation. You can't take nutrition or altitude for granted any more than you can be careless with equipment preparation.

No other sport demands such careful planning and preparation. Success in ski racing involves physical preparation in a long-term training program, and careful preparation of equipment to meet conditions on the course. But it also means considering and preparing for other factors such as variations in altitude and temperature, diet, pre- and in-race feeding, travel, fatigue, and illness.

The complications surrounding ski races are what make the sport so fascinating. Other sports have been sanitized, air conditioned, placed in a controlled environment — but not cross-country skiing. Even the spectators and race officials have to be hardy souls. I cannot prepare you for the infinite variety of conditions you may have to face. But I can provide some general principles that may help you better prepare for races and environmental extremes.

11

Diet
and Performance

Good nutrition is important for everybody, and especially athletes. It is even more important for young athletes, who need essential amino acids and other nutrients during crucial periods of growth and development. Moreover, athletes engaged in high volume training cannot do quality workouts when their energy intake is low. Serious athletes take nutrition seriously. While this chapter cannot provide a complete guide to good nutrition, it will outline ways in which you can meet your energy and nutrient needs. It should help you:

- Ensure adequate nutrition via a mixed diet;
- Understand the value of complex carbohydrates;
- Plan prerace feeds and in-race feeds;
- Determine optimal body weights and body fat for skiers.

NUTRITION

Good nutrition includes energy, essential building blocks, vitamins, minerals, and water. Energy comes predominately from carbohydrate and fat. Protein provides some energy as well as the amino acids that serve as building blocks for many tissues and compounds in the body, including muscle proteins and enzymes developed in training. Vitamins and minerals are essential in many metabolic processes,

TABLE 11.1   Daily Food Plan

Food Group	Value in Diet	Recommended Daily Intake
Milk group (milk, cheese, cottage cheese)	Protein, calcium, other minerals, and vitamins	3 or more servings (preferably low fat)
Meat group (also includes fish, fowl, nuts, peas, beans)	Protein, iron, other minerals, and B vitamins	2 or more servings (consider more fish and beans, and less meat)
Vegetables and fruits (includes potatoes)	Minerals, vitamins, and fiber	4 or more servings
Breads and cereals (includes rice and pasta)	Carbohydrate energy, protein, iron, and B vitamins, fiber	4 or more servings

and water is the amazing fluid that transports these products. You may have the impression that good nutrition is hard to achieve, that food processing, storage, and additives rob food of valuable nutrients. This isn't entirely true, however. In some respects we have access to safer, more nutritious food than ever before. The key to good nutrition is variety.

Table 11.1 provides a simple daily food plan that includes sufficient variety to meet your nutritional needs. Variety is important for this reason: When one kind of food lacks an essential nutrient, you can easily make it up in another. Nutritional problems arise when variety is lacking. In short, by selecting a mixed diet from the various food groups, you'll meet your nutritional needs.

Energy

The typical teenage athlete needs between 2000 and 3000 calories to fuel normal activities. Energy for training or competition requires additional calories. For example, a cross-country skier will burn 15-20 calories per minute or 900-1200 additional calories per hour while training. Total energy needs include basic requirements as well as those burned in vigorous activity. You lose weight if you eat less than you burn, but those of you still growing simply can't afford to regularly fall short of energy and nutrient needs.

Hungry athletes typically eat extra food to meet their extra energy needs. The extra food carries additional vitamins and minerals. Athletes who are dieting during vigorous training—and skiers often lose weight during high volume preseason training—should remember to take a vitamin supplement.

Diet. The average American diet is shown in Table 11.2. This diet is too high in fat, about right in protein for an athlete, and low in

TABLE 11.2   Average American Diet

Energy Source	% of Total Calories
Carbohydrate	40-45
Fat	40-45
Protein	15

carbohydrate. I recommend a gradual change in the composition of the diet. By substituting low fat milk for whole milk, lean meat, fish, and fowl for more fatty meat, reducing red meat intake a bit and making up the caloric difference with such complex carbohydrate as potatoes, rice, corn, beans, and whole grain products, you will approach what is called the high performance diet (see Table 11.3).

TABLE 11.3   High Performance Diet

Energy Source	% of Total Calories
Carbohydrate	60
Fat	25
Protein	15

Carbohydrate is a major source of energy. In fact, US Team skiers averaged 50% carbohydrate and ate more fat during a fall training camp, perhaps to provide fuel for long distance training. Complex carbohydrates (i.e., starches) are better than simple sugars because they include vitamins and minerals as well as energy. Fresh fruit is an excellent source of carbohydrate, but starches are better for carbohydrate loading. Fat is also an important food. It is used for cell membranes, it insulate nerves, and it builds important compounds such as hormones. Fat also is an important energy source (see Table 11.4), but we don't need as much as we usually eat, and too much fat is associated with heart disease, hypertension, and diabetes. Although growing athletes need protein, an excess will just be stored as fat. The daily food plan ensures adequate protein intake (Table 11.5 indicates some sources of protein). Again, variety in food selection is the best insurance against poor nutrition.

TABLE 11.4   Energy in Food

Source	Energy (Calories/Gram)
Fat	9.3
Carbohydrate	4.1
Protein	4.3

TABLE 11.5   Some High Protein Foods

Food	Measure	Protein (grams)
Bacon	3 strips	8.0
Beans		
and pork	1/2 cup	8.0
lima	1/2 cup	6.0
red	1/2 cup	8.0
soy	1/2 cup	10.0
Beef		
corned	3 slices	21.5
roast	2 slices	24.0
steak	1/4 pound	25.0
Biscuits	3	7.0
Cheese		
American	1 ounce	7.5
cottage	1/4 cup	7.5
Swiss	1 ounce	8.5
Chicken	3-1/2 ounces	25.0
Chili with beans	1 cup	19.0
Clams	1/2 cup	8.0
Crabmeat	5/8 cup	17.5
Egg	1 large	6.5
Fish	4 ounces	25.0
Flour		
white	1 cup	11.5
whole grain	1 cup	16.5
Ham	3-1/2 ounces	21.0
Lamb	3-1/2 ounces	22.0
Lentils	1/2 cup	8.0
Lobster	2/3 cupmeat	18.5
Macaroni and cheese	1 cup	10.0
Milk	1 cup	10.0
Peas		
split	1/2 cup	10.0
Pork		
chop	1	15.0
loin	2 slices	20.0
Pizza	1/6 of 14 inch	12.0

Nutrients

Vitamins. Vitamins are organic catalysts that help carry out important reactions, such as producing energy from carbohydrate. Without a regular supply, you can't manage these basic functions, let alone engage in vigorous activity. Vitamins come in two categories: fat soluble (A, D, E, and K) and water soluble (B and C). Extra B and C are carried off in the urine. But extra doses of *fat*-soluble vitamins are stored in fatty tissue, and they can become toxic. For this reason, you should avoid excessive vitamin intake. Table 11.6 shows the daily requirements, sources, and functions of major vitamins.

Some vitamin needs increase with extra energy expenditure. Although you can usually meet these needs with increased food intake, when you take in less food than you need, a daily vitamin supplementation may become necessary.

Minerals. A number of minerals are essential for health. Calcium and phosphorus make strong bones; magnesium and manganese help enzymes do their work. Sodium and potassium help nerves conduct and muscles contract. Iodine is needed for thyroid hormone and zinc is believed necessary for red blood cells, growth, and tissue repair (see Table 11.6).

Iron is particularly important for young athletes, both male and female. Studies on US Team members showed that several had borderline iron stores (Haymes, Puhl, and Temples, 1983). Much of the iron absorbed into the circulation goes into the production of hemoglobin in the red blood cells. The iron in hemoglobin helps carry oxygen from the lungs to the working muscles. If dietary iron intake is inadequate, the resulting anemia will have a dramatic effect on endurance performances.

Because the blood can only absorb about 10 to 20% of the iron in the diet, young athletes must take in 10 times the amount they need every day. The recommended daily allowance is 18 milligrams. Those of you who avoid meat are more likely to be iron deficient because meat is a rich source of iron. However, dates, prunes, apricots, raisins, and most beans also contain iron. If you are concerned about your iron intake, take a daily vitamin supplement *with iron*, and eat a varied diet that includes meat.

Water

Perhaps the most essential component of nutrition is the one we frequently ignore: the need for water. In this age of soda pop, coffee, tea, and other beverages, most of us never think to drink plain water. We need water every day to replace what we lose in respiration, sweat, urine, and feces. The need for extra water becomes acute when we work hard, especially in a warm climate or at higher altitude. During vigorous activity you may lose more than a liter of sweat every hour. Failure to replace the water loss will lead to serious consequences.

We get some water in the food we eat. The rest must come from fluid intake. Because thirst always underestimates fluid needs you should pay special attention to the signs of fluid loss; these include weight loss—2 pounds for each quart, and a small volume of concentrated urine. Be alert to these signs, and don't return to practice until your fluid level is where it should be.

TABLE 11.6   Vitamins and Minerals: Needs, Sources, Functions

	Recommended* Daily Allowance	Some Sources	Importance
Vitamin			
Fat Soluble			
A	5000/4000 (IU)	Liver, milk products	Resistance to infection; light adaptation
D	400 (IU)	Sunlight, eggs, fish, milk products	Calcium absorption
E	15/12 (IU)	Vegetable oils, greens	Cell function
Water Soluble			
C	45 (mg)	Citrus fruits, tomatoes	Blood vessels, connective tissue, stress
Folacin	400 (µg)	Greens, liver	Red blood cells
Niacin	20/14 (mg)	Peanuts, grains, greens, poultry, fish	Energy production
Riboflavin (B$_2$)	1.8/1.4 (mg)	Milk, eggs, fish, meat, greens	Energy production
Thiamin (B$_1$)	1.5/1.1 (mg)	Meat, grains, milk	Energy production
B$_6$	2.0 (mg)	Grains, meat, bananas, lima beans	Energy, protein, hemoglobin
B$_{12}$	3.0 (µg)	Liver, clams, fish	Red blood cells, energy, nervous system
Mineral			
Calcium	1200 (mg)	Milk products, green leafy vegetables	Bones, muscles, blood
Phosphorous	1200 (mg)	Liver, fish, meat, beans, milk	Bones, blood, cells
Iodine	150/115 (µg)	Seafood, iodized salt	Thyroid hormone
Iron	18 (mg)	Liver, meat, beans, dried fruit	Oxygen binding in blood and muscle
Magnesium	400/300 (mg)	Grains, nuts, beans, green leafy vegetables	Enzymes and energy production
Zinc	15 (mg)	Shellfish, grains, meat	Healing, growth, blood cell production

*Designed to maintain good nutrition in healthy people. Covers variations among most normal individuals under usual environmental stresses (National Research Council). When two numbers are given, the first refers to the recommended daily allowance for boys, the second to that for girls.

DIET AND PERFORMANCE

Carbohydrate Loading

Carbohydrate loading is a proven method of raising muscle glycogen levels to ensure energy availability for longer races. Carbohydrate loading won't make you ski faster, but it will help you maintain a fast pace longer. Athletes on the performance diet usually have over 20 grams of glycogen per kilogram of muscle, enough for races up to 1 hour long. So ski races that last less than 1 hour do not require special attention to carbohydrate; just taper practice a couple of days before the race and be sure to get enough carbohydrate. The two loading schemes that follow are for events lasting over 1 hour.

One to Two Hours. Four days before the event ski a long, hard workout to deplete muscle glycogen stores (see Figure 11.1). This activates an enzyme responsible for packing glycogen in the muscle. Next, raise your carbohydrate intake for the next few days by adding extra starches and sugar treats (fruit sugar or fructose doesn't work as well) to your regular diet. Drink lots of water since carbohydrates are stored with water. You may gain a little weight but you will also

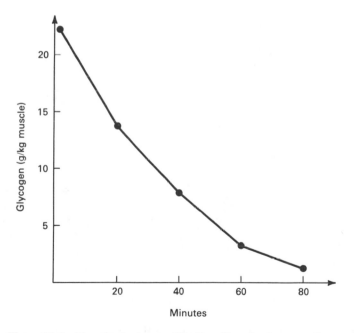

Figure 11.1   Muscle glycogen utilization. Muscle glycogen stores become depleted after about 80 minutes of vigorous effort. Carbohydrate loading will provide enough glycogen to last a 50-km ski marathon.

double your muscle glycogen stores. Of course, you should taper training so you won't burn up the glycogen before the race.

Over Two Hours. Events lasting over 2 hours may require even more glycogen, so do your depletion effort 6 days before the big event. Ski another depletion workout the following day. On both days keep your carbohydrate intake down. After the second depletion go back on a high carbohydrate intake, with water and vitamins, and taper your training. This technique has raised glycogen stores as much as three to four times over normal levels. In lab studies, best endurance performances are *always* recorded when glycogen levels are high. However, you should know that some athletes can't tolerate this double depletion technique, and some of the world's great endurance athletes forego any special attempt to carbohydrate load, relying instead on their regularly high carbohydrate diet. Start with the 4-day approach to see if you like it. If you do, then you might try the double depletion technique for a marathon in the Great American Ski Chase Series. Finally, let me emphasize that glycogen loaded in one muscle cannot be used in another. Therefore, if you want to load skiing muscles, you must first deplete them, then follow with increased carbohydrate intake.

Precompetition Meal

Generally speaking, you should eat the precompetition meal that works for you. Just be sure you eat it at least 3 hours before the event so you have a relatively empty stomach at race time. Avoid difficult-to-digest fats and excess protein. Most athletes tolerate what they normally eat, so long as they don't overdo. Especially nervous athletes are usually able to tolerate balanced and palatable liquid meals.

Endurance Events. Some athletes choose not to eat before competition, especially for races that start in the morning. Although reason might suggest another high carbohydrate meal before a long race, the research doesn't agree. A high sugar meal like pancakes with Vermont maple syrup provokes insulin release, and the insulin speeds the uptake of sugar into the muscles. Thus, the muscles begin the event using a high proportion of carbohydrate. Fasting athletes are more likely to use more fat, thereby conserving muscle glycogen for use later in the event.

Sports physiologist Dave Costill has shown that two cups of coffee in the hour before an endurance test stimulates fat mobilization and utilization in the early stages of the effort. This too conserves limited stores of muscle glycogen. But don't drink coffee unless you are familiar with its effects. It may make you overly nervous, and its strong diuretic effect will make you run to a rest room before the start.

Generally, the excitement of competition will probably release enough adrenalin to mobilize the fat energy you need.

If not eating before competition makes you feel weak, eat a light, easily digested meal several hours before the start. I have found that my usual peanut butter and honey sandwich — on whole wheat bread with nonhydrogenated peanut butter — works well for me. I am used to it, it is easily digested, and it doesn't leave me feeling hungry and weak. Another favorite is pancakes plus an egg to slow the entry of glucose into the system. But more important than what you eat before the event may be what you eat during the race.

In-Race Feeding

Extra fuel isn't necessary during such events as 5, 10, or 15 km races. If you are only going to drive around the block you don't need a full tank of gas. Feeding becomes important when competition stretches out over many hours, as in races of 30 km and above. Then it is essential to replace your fluid and maintain energy and blood sugar levels.

Fluids. On warmer days or when you misjudge the temperature and wear a racing suit that is too warm, fluid loss can rival that experienced in summer months. Furthermore, races at higher elevations lead to considerable fluid loss in the expired air. So you must replace fluids or your performance will suffer. Drink a cup or two of water before the race, and drink at every aid station along the course. Commercial sport ades are fine, but it is more important to get water than salt. A good compromise is to drink one cup of ade for one of water. Incidentally, racers have used caffeine (as in defizzed pop) as a pick-me-up in long events. Caffeine use may soon be limited or banned in international competition, however.

Energy. Sometime after 80 minutes of vigorous effort, when muscle glycogen levels become depleted (see Figure 2.1), the muscles turn to blood sugar for added energy. The liver can only carry about 80 grams of carbohydrate, so when liver glycogen is exhausted and blood sugar levels drop, your race is over. You may be able to finish using fat as a fuel, but you won't have a competitive pace. And some individuals suffer symptoms such as exhaustion, dizziness, blurred vision, and headaches when blood glucose levels decline. The loss of motivation such symptoms produce often causes racers to drop out of the competition. And low blood sugar, in combination with exhaustion and rapid cooling, can lead to life-threatening hypothermia, as discussed in Chapter 12.

Therefore, you must replace energy in addition to fluid at feeding stations. One approach is to lace your drink with sugar; however, data on road runners suggests that too much sugar (over 25 grams per liter) slows the passage of fluid *or* sugar into the bloodstream. Skiers seem to tolerate higher sugar levels in their replacement drinks, perhaps because their movements are smoother and the temperatures cooler than in running. Commercial sport ades often carry about 50 grams of glucose per liter of drink. In ski marathons many racers like to take solid food such as cookies, oranges, or bananas, and some are known to drink a sweet drink laced with blueberries. Being somewhat prone to hypoglycemia or low blood sugar, I need all the help I can get in long races, and that means drinks, solid food, even hard candy to suck on. In-race feeding is a personal matter and each racer must learn what works best for him or her. But remember, when fluid intake is crucial, lower your sugar concentration. For long races and on cooler days, you can increase sugar concentration and even take solid food for adequate energy.

After Competition

At the end of a race you'll need to replace the fluid and energy you lost — but do it slowly. Too much too soon will lead to cramps, nausea, and a prolonged recovery; take your time and you'll be ready to go again in a day or so. Check your weight to estimate fluid loss: a 6-pound weight loss means you still need to replace 3 quarts of water. Because thirst always underestimates fluid needs, continue fluid replacement after you have satisfied your thirst.

Concentrate on carbohydrate to replace energy stores in the liver and muscles. Adequate portions of good quality protein and vitamin supplements enable tissues to repair themselves rapidly. With a day or two of rest, you'll be ready to resume your training schedule. Some events call for successive days of demanding effort. Minnesota's Finlandia Ski Marathon challenges athletes with back-to-back 50 kilometer (31 mile) races. Some skiers seem surprisingly able to replace their energy stores overnight and come back with good performances on the second day. Of course, this is only true for some athletes. Recovery is an individual characteristic.* Some need more time than others. If you do, admit it and give yourself the rest you need.

BODY WEIGHT AND PERFORMANCE

While in distance running extra weight can be a handicap, this isn't necessarily true in skiing. In ski racing extra fat is merely insulation while additional muscle can contribute to performance. Some fat is needed to provide insulation against the cold, but excess fat does not

---

*Slow-twitch muscle seems to replace resting stores of glycogen in 24 hours; there is evidence that older athletes take longer to replace muscle glycogen stores.

contribute to performance. Men on the US Ski Team carry 4-7% of their weight as fat, whereas women on the team range between 12 and 17%. Extra fat is a burden that must be carried up hills. Hard working skiers usually burn off any excess in the months preceding the competitive season. Use inexpensive skinfold calipers and the chart in Appendix A to estimate your percent body fat. If you need to lose weight, do it slowly by increasing caloric expenditure through exercise and by decreasing caloric intake. Your weight loss program should begin months before the competitive season, because weight loss shouldn't exceed 1-2 pounds per week during hard training.

SUMMARY

- Follow the High Performance Diet*

Carbohydrate	60% of calories
Fat	25%
Protein	15%

- Eat a variety of foods from the four food groups.
- Always drink plenty of water and fruit juices.
- Determine a good racing weight and percentage of fat and achieve it with 1 to 2 lbs weight loss per week.
- Use a daily vitamin supplement, with iron, if you are losing weight while training.

*Incidentally, a recent study has shown that endurance athletes can adapt to and perform well on a high fat diet. While this is a fascinating bit of physiology that illustrates how remarkably adaptable we are, I do not recommend a high fat diet because of the extreme health consequences, including high blood cholesterol and metabolic acidosis. The High Performance Diet is good for performance *and* health.

12

Environment
and Performance

Changes in temperature affect more than the wax on your skis; they influence the racers as well. Although warm temperatures usually are not considered a problem, all skiers need to know how to handle extremes of heat or cold. Year-round training means that skiers train during the summer, and the increasing popularity of roller ski races will lure some into heat stress conditions. You and your coach must know how to adjust or acclimatize to the rigors of heat, cold, and altitude. You also need to know how to avoid the problems associated with exercise in polluted atmospheres.

This chapter should help you:

- Avoid environmental problems;
- Acclimatize to heat, cold, and altitude.

HEAT

When you exercise in a hot climate, body temperature rises higher than it would for the exercise alone. Eventually, we begin to sweat, our major defense against the heat. Sweat evaporates from the skin, and this evaporation cools the body. But when the humidity is high the sweat doesn't evaporate; it just drips off the body and no heat is lost. The fluid we lose through sweat must be replaced or we risk, along with dehydration and diminished performance, the possibility of heat stress disorders. *Heat cramps* are a nuisance that can be treated with lightly salted water or commercial sport drinks and stretching. *Heat exhaustion* due to dehydration requires rest and fluid replacement. *Heat stroke* is a total collapse of the temperature-regulating mechanism. It is a life-threatening emergency that requires medical assistance. Exposure to heat should never reach this critical point, and it won't if you pay adequate attention to fluid replacement fitness and acclimatization.

Prevention

You can prevent heat stress problems and better cope with hot climates in two ways: through fitness and acclimatization. First, a high level of fitness is one of the best ways to protect against heat stress. Fit athletes have a well-developed circulatory capacity and increased blood volume, and both are important for the regulation of body temperature. Fit people exercise with lower heart rates. They start to sweat sooner, thereby maintaining a lower body temperature. Highly fit athletes adjust or acclimatize to exercise in the heat twice as fast as unfit individuals. They lose their acclimatization more slowly, and are able to regain it rapidly when exposed again to the heat.

Acclimatization is a gradual adjustment to exercise in the heat. You can become acclimatized by gradually increasing your exercise in a hot environment for four successive days. You should cut your training 40% the first day, and reduce it 30, 20, and 10% on the second, third, and fourth days respectively. Make sure you have water available at all times and use the salt shaker with meals—but only for the duration of the heat exposure. During extended exposures, take care to replace potassium losses with citrus fruits, bananas, and other potassium-rich foods.

Avoid excess heat by training in the morning or evening, and by wearing a minimum of light-colored clothing. Never venture out to train without a water bottle. Ask your coach to carry extra water for those of you who forget. Even though these guidelines will enable you to better train or compete in the heat, this kind of environment always takes its toll; so, adjust your training goals on extremely hot days or when the humidity is high. Keep track of your morning weight (after toilet, before breakfast) and don't train if your weight is more than 2 lbs, or 1 quart, below the previous day's weight, indicating inadequate fluid replacement. Finally, remember that everyone tolerates heat differently; pay attention to *your* own tolerance, work at *your* pace, and take breaks when *you* need them.

COLD

Skiers are familiar with the dangers of cold exposure—wind chill, frostbite, and hypothermia. Wind chill is inevitable in skiing because downhills create their own chill. Skiers soon learn to protect vulnerable parts from frostbite with extra layers of clothing and other devices. In shorter races, the risk of chill or frostbite is minimal due to the tremendous amount of heat generated in skiing. In longer races, exposed noses, cheeks, and ear lobes must be protected carefully. And light gloves, racing suits, and shoes may become inadequate if the temperature drops unexpectedly.

In distance races, inexperienced racers are exposed longer; they are more likely to be fatigued, to have lowered blood glucose and rapid cooling of wet clothing—all of which predisposes them to hypothermia. Hypothermia is a collapse of the temperature-regulating mechanism, manifested first by confusion and slurred speech, then fatigue and a desire to strip off clothing and sleep in the snow. Hypothermia is a life-threatening emergency that can best be treated in a well-equipped medical facility. If you find a skier in this condition, keep the victim as warm as possible and rush him or her to medical assistance. Don't waste valuable time by trying to rewarm the victim—unless help is too far away. The way to avoid the problem is to eat often, avoiding excess perspiration, and quit a race or hard practice before the problem becomes an emergency. Unfortunately, once you become hypothermic, you can't think clearly and may need to be pulled off the course. Keep alert to this problem in yourself and other skiers.

Prevention

You can reduce the risks of cold exposure in several ways. Adequate clothing, with wind protection when necessary, is the most obvious measure. One often-forgotten and very important protector is a hat. Cold causes blood vessels in the skin to constrict in order to avoid excess heat loss; however, blood vessels in the head don't constrict. Without a hat, then, you will suffer considerable heat loss. A light hat made of polypropylene will protect your head and wick perspiration from the skin.

The excess exposure in long races may cause muscles to cool and become less efficient, so you need to be ready to add clothing when the mercury falls. Don't put a lot of heavy clothing on too soon, however, or you will sweat and become a candidate for rapid cooling and hypothermia. Select underwear that wicks perspiration to the surface. Use a nylon or Gore Tex windbreaker to protect your trunk and groin from rapid cooling and frostbite. Carry extra clothing, including an extra hat, for longer races or be certain extra clothing is available if and when you need it. Don't ruin a race by being unprepared.*

Once again, the other protection against cold is acclimatization — or rather, adaptation. Although we may not really acclimatize to the cold, we certainly do adapt. We seem to learn to tolerate cold better — witness those racers who participate without gloves when the temperature is well below freezing. Again, some individuals adjust better than others. Some become quite tolerant to the cold while a few never adjust (see Table 12.1).

A few older skiers will have a problem called Raynaud's disease, a severe cold-induced constriction of blood vessels in the fingertips. Although constriction is common in the cold it usually abates as the body warms, allowing blood to return to the fingers. This doesn't occur with the Raynaud's sufferers, who experience intense pain from the constriction. Fortunately, researchers at the US Army Environmental Research Institute in Natick, Massachusetts, have developed a treatment that reduces or eliminates the problem without drugs or surgery. Sufferers merely expose their lightly clothed bodies to the cold while immersing their fingers in hot water. Done several times a day for 3 weeks, the treatment fools the vessels into dilation and eliminates the problem.

Finally, remember that dehydration is a problem in the winter as well as the summer. Carry a water bottle to practice and use it (for health reasons never drink from a friend's bottle unless an emergency arises). When your workout is over, strip off your wet clothing and *immediately* put on some dry ones. After a hard workout or race, avoid crowds; your immunologic system or resistance is less efficient after exhaustive effort. Studies on US Team members show that the salivary immunoglobulins, the first line of defense against upper respiratory infection, are depressed after a race. Remember, the upper respiratory infection is the Achilles heel of the ski racer.

ALTITUDE

Ski races often take place on or near mountains, so altitude is often an important factor in preparation and performance. Although major national race courses may not exceed 1650 meters (5400 ft) in elevation, many important regional races and several ski marathons take place above that elevation. You and your coach should know how to prepare for races held at moderate altitudes (1500-2500 meters,

---

*Cold hands usually rewarm when protected from the cold; but blood flow only returns to frigid feet when the body temperature (core) is raised. Use booties (ski muffs) to protect the feet when temperatures drop.

TABLE 12.1 Wind Chill Chart

Wind Speed in MPH	Actual Thermometer Reading (°F)											
	50	40	30	20	10	0	−10	−20	−30	−40	−50	−60
						Equivalent Temperature (°F)						
Calm	50	40	30	20	10	0	−10	−20	−30	−40	−50	−60
5	48	37	27	16	6	−5	−15	−26	−36	−47	−57	−68
10	40	28	16	4	−9	−21	−33	−46	−58	−70	−83	−95
15	36	22	9	−5	−18	−36	−45	−58	−72	−85	−99	−112
20	32	18	4	−10	−25	−39	−53	−67	−82	−96	−110	−124
25	30	16	0	−15	−29	−44	−59	−74	−88	−104	−118	−133
30	28	13	−2	−18	−33	−48	−63	−79	−94	−109	−125	−140
35	27	11	−4	−20	−35	−49	−67	−82	−98	−113	−129	−145
40	26	10	−6	−21	−37	−53	−69	−85	−100	−116	−132	−148

(Wind speeds greater than 40 MPH have little additional effect)

LITTLE DANGER (for properly clothed person)

INCREASING DANGER

GREAT DANGER

Danger from freezing of exposed flesh

From Sharkey, 1974.

5000-8000 ft). And some of you will want to know how to use altitude training to improve performance at lower elevations.

Going Up

The lowlander moving to a higher elevation for competition has two choices: (a) arrive and compete as soon as possible, or (b) arrive early and acclimatize to altitude. Since less oxygen is available at higher elevations, performance in ski races will always be more difficult there. Training at that altitude will diminish but never eliminate the effects. Some athletes become listless and lose their appetite at higher elevations; they may do better by competing soon after they arrive. If you decide to arrive early and acclimatize, allow approximately a week for each 1000 ft above 5000 ft elevation. Thus, for a ski marathon in Colorado, which has an 8000-ft elevation, you should leave home and train for 3 weeks at the elevation of the race.

Acclimatization

Little useful acclimatization takes place without training. Avoid the tendency to slow down all aspects of training while at altitude. Instead, shorten your distances to maintain some pace training. You could even travel to a lower elevation 2 days each week to do long interval or pace training. And watch out for signs of overtraining, dehydration, and weight loss.

The altitude exposure and training will have several effects. It will lead to an increased ability to take in air and an increase in red blood cells and hemoglobin. You'll also have increased small blood vessels or capillaries and muscle myoglobin. All of these changes improve your ability to take in, transport, and utilize oxygen, thereby partially compensating for reduced oxygen in the atmosphere. Once again, however, these well-documented changes reduce but never eliminate the effects of altitude on performance. But while training and acclimatization at altitude will improve performance at that specific altitude, the effects of altitude training for performance at lower elevations is less well-established.

Altitude Training

Research in this area fails to support the time and effort many spend in an attempt to ski better at low elevations. Only a few studies show improved performance upon return to a lower elevation. Yet in spite of this, many athletes and coaches are convinced altitude training has a positive effect. Why the discrepancy between research and experience? It may be that the research on altitude training has missed the individual response by looking at group results.

But what differentiates individuals in respect to altitude training? Inspection of the blood profiles for various skiers suggests one possibility. Those with relatively low red blood cell, hemoglobin, and iron counts may profit, whereas those with high values may not. Raising hemoglobin levels above 17 or 18 grams per 100 ml blood (16 is average for men, 14 for women) may just make the blood thicker and hard to pump. Skiers with values of around 14 grams/dl for men and 12 for women may be the ones who profit from the exposure to altitude. Those with average values may be the ones who do about the same. Sport physiologists will be testing this hypothesis to determine who does and who doesn't need exposure to altitude. In the meantime, don't look at altitude exposure as a sure-fire way to improve your endurance (see Table 12.2).

Three weeks of altitude training at 2250 meters will raise hemoglobin levels about 2 grams. On return to lower elevations these hemoglobin and red blood cell levels begin to return to prealtitude values. Why does this increase help some and not others? Perhaps because thicker blood (i.e., with higher red blood cell and hemoglobin levels) can flow more easily, since blood vessels dilate when oxygen supply is limited. This dilation doesn't occur at lower elevations, so the thicker blood may just be hard to pump. Those with low values are raised into the normal range, aiding oxygen transport without the burden of overly viscous blood.

TABLE 12.2   Altitude Training Guidelines

At altitude, maintain sea level pace during prolonged intense Anaerobic Threshold (AT) training. Adjust by shortening the duration of work intervals and lengthening active rest periods. Increase the number of work bouts to keep total work equal to the low elevation workload.

For longer training efforts work at a level of exertion similar (subjectively) to the low elevation pace. Total training load (hours, kilometers, miles) can be maintained at altitude.

OR

Schedule 2-3 workouts/week at a lower elevation to conduct Anaerobic Threshold (AT) training (pace, long intervals, fast distance). Anaerobic or speed training can be conducted at altitude.

Adaptation Period for Performance at Altitude

Recommended guidelines for acclimatization periods prior to competitive events:

1. A minimum period of 14 days for competitions up to 2000 meters.
2. 21 days for competitions between 2000 and 2500 meters.
3. 28 days for competitions organized above 2500 meters.

If unable to spend prolonged periods for acclimatization prior to competition, arrive at altitude just prior to the competitive event.

There is another possibility, of course: Research shows that about one-third of the subjects in a study will be subject to a *placebo* effect. That is, this one-third will perceive an effect if one is strongly suggested. Performance does feel easier upon return to a lower elevation, and if it feels easier, some athletes may be willing to try harder, believing in the value of altitude training. Whatever the case, skiing feels easier at 1000 meters after you've been at 2000 meters, but probably not much easier than it was before you went off for altitude training.

Coming Down

If you are coming down from altitude to perform, the best bet is to compete soon after you arrive. The special benefits of altitude—if they exist—soon fade at lower elevations. The native of higher altitude, that is, above 3000 meters, may want to come down sooner and do tempo work, which is difficult with a limited oxygen supply.

Related Issues. Altitude simulators and blood doping are related to altitude training. The simulators (see Figure 12.1) reduce the oxygen content of the inspired air to simulate a higher elevation. Athletes soon tire of the devices and prefer instead to head for the hills. Blood doping consists of the removal of about 1000 cc of blood which is then stored for subsequent reinfusion of the red cells to simulate altitude training effects. Most athletes frown on unnatural approaches to improved performance, preferring instead to seek success based on natural endowment and hard work.

In General

While at altitude pay special attention to fluids, diet, and rest. You breathe more and lose more water vapor in this environment, so take the water bottle to all training sessions and take fluids during races. Eat extra carbohydrate since the body prefers that fuel when oxygen supply is limited. And be sure to get extra rest to compensate for the added stress of altitude. All aspects of training are harder, and rest and sleep are often difficult. So schedule more rest breaks, short sessions, and off days. And keep records to try and see if you profit from altitude training when you return to lower elevations.

AIR POLLUTION

Why worry about air pollution when ski races are held in clear mountain air? Because you are exposed to pollution in some forms of training, and those of you who are more sensitive may carry the effects of asthma or allergies into competition. Air pollution can irritate airways and provoke bronchitis, cause alveolar breakdown in the

(a)

(b)

(c)

Figure 12.1 US Team member Tim Caldwell tries out an altitude simulator (a & b). Tim eventually chose to altitude train the natural way (c) as pictured during a 25-mile workout in Montana's Glacier National Park. In part a of this figure, Tim is wearing his heart rate monitor. The arm band is used to reduce the shock of pole plant on his "tennis elbow."

lungs—a condition called emphysema, reduce oxygen-carrying capacity with carbon monoxide, and cause or contribute to major diseases such as cancer and heart disease. So while it makes good sense to avoid pollution, it makes especially good sense to avoid air pollution during exercise; the increased air intake increases exposure.

Although you can't always avoid air pollution, you can at least minimize your exposure to it. Most skiers are hardy souls who pride themselves on their independence and self-sufficiency, and they are likely to cut and burn firewood to heat their homes, cabins, and saunas. Unfortunately, wood smoke contains respirable carcinogens just as cigarettes do. When atmospheric conditions are poor, for example, during air inversions, mountain valley towns trap air and pollution levels rise. That is the time to stop burning and to do your training elsewhere.

SUMMARY

Anticipate the effects of the environment and prepare for them. Acclimatize gradually, wear proper clothing, and avoid extremes in temperature. People often ask me if lung tissue will freeze in extremely cold weather. The answer is no, it won't. Early season cold exposure may dry the lungs with deep breathing of cold dry air, but the ensuing cough is only a sign of dryness, not freezing. The human respiratory apparatus is a great air conditioner that warms and humidifies air before it reaches the sacs of the lungs. But that doesn't mean training or competition in extremely cold air is fun—it isn't. I prefer to stay inside when the temperature and wind chill exceed $-20°F$ ($-29°C$). Ski down a hill at 25 miles per hour on a -20 day and the equivalent temperature (wind chill) drops to -74 degrees. The equivalent temperature describes the rate at which heat is lost from the body. So be sensible about environmental extremes; and you coaches and race directors, consider the athlete's health, safety, and enjoyment of skiing when you make decisions about races.

Preparation and Performance

You may consider performance to be synonymous with competition, and to an extent they are similar. But they don't actually mean the same thing. While both imply putting on a racing suit, tying on a number, and going for it, the connotations of each are different. Competitors are more concerned with winning and losing, with the final outcome. Performers, on the other hand, attach secondary importance to winning, evaluating their performance against a goal or ideal. Performers feel that winning against a lesser opponent isn't a big deal, that coming in second is less important than achieving a personal best.

This chapter is about performance and how to prepare for it. One way to begin is to start thinking like a performer. Focus on the quality of skiing and the experience, not the final outcome. Seek out good competition because it improves your performance. Realize that you can't always be a winner but you can become a consistent performer. And when you do the medals and ribbons will take care of themselves.

This chapter will help you:

- Plan and prepare for consistent performances;
- Recognize common performance problems;
- Identify and avoid problems of stress and overtraining.

PREPARATION FOR PERFORMERS

Goals

Preparation begins before your first training session; it starts with the establishment of short- and long-term goals. Short-term goals like hours of daily and weekly training, time per kilometer in pace workouts, strength and power objectives, and distance or vertical targets set the stage for future performances. If you achieve the short-term goals, you're more likely to achieve the long-term ones. Long-term goals include annual hours or kilometers of training, minutes per kilometer in races, improved race times and personal records, completing distance races in good form, making regional or national teams, and so forth.

Begin with attainable goals, meet them, and then set higher ones. As you achieve your goals, you'll gain confidence, satisfaction, fitness, and technique. You may never finish first but you can still be a winner. Cross-country skiing is a long-term enterprise; it takes years for champions to develop and mature. So you and your coach must share a long view; you both must learn to enjoy the present as you prepare for the future. If you look only at the future, if you are never satisfied because your long-term goals are perpetually out of reach, then you very well may grow frustrated with skiing and quit. It would be a shame, too, because this sport has so much to offer to so many.

Keeping Records. Seasonal training goals are reached one day at a time, and you should keep records of that progress. The weekly training log shown in Appendix D provides space for recording your energy and muscular training along with some of your subjective feelings. Begin now to keep track of your progress. Psychologists recognize the value of record keeping as a source of feedback and motivation. Being able to see what you have done reinforces appropriate behaviors, making it more likely that you'll stick to training. Of course, you'll get other sorts of feedback as you participate: the enjoyment of training with friends, the sense of improvement, success in races. But smart athletes use everything possible to keep on schedule. If the snow is bad or your training partner is sick or out of town, will you still go out and train? You will if your training log stares you in the face every day. Success in sport—and in life for that matter—goes to the persistent, determined, unrelenting individuals who have a goal and keep it in sight.

So set goals and keep track of your progress. If injury or illness set you back, adjust your sights and get back to work—it happens to everyone. If your goals are reasonable, you should still be able to reach them.

Psychological Preparation

Psyching Up. A ski race provides all the motivation most of us can stand; we don't need additional arousal. The trick is to perform well in spite of the emotional tension, and that involves careful mental preparation—relaxation and concentration, for example. Hormones like adrenalin are secreted before and during competition. They help mobilize energy and prepare the cardiovascular system for extreme effort. If the thrill and challenge of competition don't provoke the secretions, no pep talk will help. Most athletes are excited and aroused and need to learn ways to control that emotion before and during the competition—too much arousal hurts a skilled performance. If you are like most athletes, then, you need to learn and practice psychological skills such as those that follow:

- *Relaxation.* You must become relaxed and uncritical so your body can perform the skills it has learned. Practice relaxation at home. Then while training, say "easy" on your exhale, focus on your rhythmic breathing, and let the movement flow. Continue to practice the skill in early races.

- *Activation.* This is the opposite of relaxation; you need it when you have to be pepped up during a long, grueling race. Use emotionally charged words such as punch, pump, drive, charge, power, or blast up hills. Tense muscles, squeeze pole grips, slap tired parts back to life. Think of the race's importance and say "go" to yourself on every exhale.

- *Concentration.* Don't let your mind wander or disassociate during a race. Learn to focus on the signals coming from your body. Are you working too hard, not hard enough? Monitor your technique and adjust if necessary. Keep track of your competitors as well; when you lose track of your form or the opposition your pace will suffer. And when things get tense or tough—relax.

- *Imagery.* Visualize yourself performing in good form, mentally practice specific skills and movements. See yourself as a successful performer.

These and other psychological skills cannot be learned overnight. They require years of practice if they are to be used successfully in the heat of competition. Start now to master the skills that will help you or your athletes do their best in every race.*

*For more information on psychological skills and how to learn them, see Terry Orlick, *In Pursuit of Excellence* (Champaign, IL: Human Kinetics Publishers, 1980).

Physiological Preparation

Both forms of preparation, psychological and physiological, should be gauged to reach a peak before the most important part of the season. Decide when you want to peak and how long the peak will have to last. Remember that peaks are short-lived, few last more than a month. If your season calls for important qualifier races in December and big events in late February and March, plan on peaking twice. Between peaks you can continue to compete, but not with the same degree of physical and mental intensity.

Physical preparation begins 6 to 8 weeks before the peak period of the season. Some athletes take longer than others. Peaking involves the final tuning of the engine, getting the last little bit out of the anaerobic energy pathways while maintaining aerobic capabilities. Maximum benefits are accomplished in 6 to 8 weeks, so this phase of training should never be prolonged. Too much of this high intensity effort will wear down the strongest of athletes.

During the peaking period concentrate on good technique. Never use sloppy form during interval or pace work. When you lose your form, terminate that phase of the workout. Use early races to sharpen the quality of your performance; don't worry about winning them. In addition, work on speed, taper the volume of training, and get lots of rest. Eat sensibly and keep track of your weight, using the last few weeks to achieve your best competitive weight.

Use the week prior to a big race for building muscle glycogen stores. Carbohydrate load if the race calls for it, but try not to gain more than 2 pounds.

Taper training several days before an important event. Do easy stretching and form work in the days preceding competition. Avoid drug use, including aspirin and antihistamines, and stimulants like coffee or tea the night before the race. Try for a normal night's sleep. If you are too excited to fall asleep, don't fret, you are still getting needed rest. If possible, use the relaxation technique to help you sleep.

On race day arise early to allow time for eating, personal hygiene, and care of equipment. Do you have physical problems like blisters that need attention? Do you need medication? Do your boots need laces? Check bindings to be sure they are firmly affixed to the skis. In short, leave nothing to chance. Get out early so you'll have time to warm up adequately and to test your wax. And be prepared for things that change, like the weather. Carry food energy, extra wax, a wind breaker, and a dry hat for long races. Don't be like my friend Mike, who got a late start in a ski marathon when he realized his racing bib number was back at the motel. And one final matter — check to be sure your boots are securely fixed in the bindings. I once started in the midst of a mass start only to lose a ski in the first hundred yards. By the time I got it back on I was in the back of the pack.

PERFORMANCE PROBLEMS

Those of us who train are often beset with minor and occasionally major problems, most of which are avoidable. The problems we fail to prevent can usually be solved with a common-sense cure, such as ice or rest. Some are serious enough to require a rehabilitation program.

Prevention

The best approach to most problems is to avoid them. Smart athletes anticipate problems and take steps to prevent them.

Soreness. Muscle soreness can be prevented or minimized by easing into a new season and keeping muscles and joints warm during the early weeks of practice. Don't do any all-out ballistic (rapid, forceful) movements in the early days of practice. And always stretch before and after practice.

Blisters. Experienced distance athletes avoid blisters and lost toenails by using a skin lubricant on toes and feet. I never hike, run, or cross-country ski without a dab of petroleum jelly. Incidentally, other areas of the body benefit from a dab of lubricant, especially during long workouts on hot days.

Another form of prevention is a piece of moleskin on the heel or other problem areas. If vaseline, tube socks, or two pairs of socks won't stop blister formation, the area should be covered before activity. When applied with tincture of benzoine (tuf skin), a strip of moleskin will stay in place for a long workout or race. It may even outlast several showers.

At the *first* hint of a blister, cover the skin with moleskin or a large bandage. Advanced cases can be treated with a sterilized hollow needle. Release the fluid, treat with antiseptic, cover with gauze, circle with foam rubber, and go back to work. Your coach should keep the items needed for prevention and treatment handy, especially on road trips. Be sure you take a prevention kit on back country hiking and ski tours also.

Treatment

When exercise problems such as shin splints or sore knees arise, we usually give all our attention to treatment. But it is wise to consider the reason for the problem so you can learn from mistakes. Worn out shoes often cause injuries. Wear patterns on running shoes help show why problems arise. Structural problems in the foot can cause foot, ankle, knee, hip, or even back problems. So find out the cause of the problem while it's being treated. You'll soon become an expert in the treatment of minor ailments. But remember, major problems deserve professional attention. See an athletic trainer for help; if the trainer can't help you, he or she will refer you to the professional who can. Perhaps a podiatrist can solve your foot problems with an orthotic (foot support). Consider surgery only after other solutions have been considered, and when several physicians agree on the approach.

For most minor sprains and strains all you need is *ICE*. That is,

- Ice
- Compression
- Elevation

Use ice for the first 3 days after a sprain. When used with compression and elevation, ice will cure most problems in a few days. More serious sprains may also require contrast bathing (cold/heat) after the first 3 days. The best way to apply ice is also the most painful, the slush bucket. Also effective is a plastic bag of crushed ice. Use a frozen popsicle or a tongue depressor frozen in a can for spot treatments of bruises, tendons, and ligaments.

Compression, which prevents further swelling, is achieved with an elastic bandage wrapped firmly but not too tightly around the sprain. Then elevate the area as much as possible to help drain excess fluid. With the *ICE* treatment, you will be back in action quickly.

Once sprained, an ankle or knee will always be somewhat weaker, no matter how much you exercise to strengthen it. You can use tape to protect an ankle from further injury, but that takes time and money. Another approach is to return to high-cut shoes for back country workouts. Many athletes find they can get the support they need with high-cut shoes or with a reusable ankle corset. These lace-on canvas ankle supports provide the support of tape without the bother.

REHABILITATION

Early ambulation is the key to successful rehabilitation. That means movement and weight bearing as soon as pain and swelling subside. A decade ago, a knee operation meant a cast and a long rehabilitation period. Today, many operations are performed through a small viewing tube called an arthroscope. You will be able to walk home afterward and regain full movement quickly because you won't get the adhesions that form when a joint can't move.

As soon as possible after an injury or operation, begin a reconditioning program. Athletes usually concentrate on developing only strength after an operation. When the injured limb is as strong as the uninjured limb, they consider rehabilitation complete. However, that is definitely *not* the case.

When you've restored your strength, you should start working on muscle endurance. A strong muscle without endurance will fatigue quickly and be susceptible to further injury. Do numerous repetitions to return endurance to pre-injury levels. For example, after strength has been restored to thigh muscles, use a bicycle to bring back needed endurance. Remember, rehabilitation isn't complete until range of motion, strength, and endurance are normal. And since skiing calls for power you had better add some of that as well.

Don't even consider a return to competition until your rehabilitation is complete. Let your body be your guide; if it hurts, don't use it.

ILLNESS

Do your best to defend yourself against infection; keep your resistance as high as possible. You need lots of rest and sleep and a sound diet. Avoid stress when training hard and be alert to the signs of overtraining. When infection does strike, be it viral or bacterial, stop training until the fever, achy muscles, and weakness are gone. Only after the fever is gone for a full 24 hours without the aid of aspirin should you return to vigorous activity. Modify training until you feel strong again; get extra rest, drink lots of fluids, and take vitamin C if you want to. Remember, if you go back too fast, you may be a candidate for a long-lasting illness.

Infections that last more than a few days, especially when they include a severe sore throat or cough or considerable pain, call for a visit to the doctor. When sinus or throat problems last for weeks and weeks, you should consider possible allergies. Many athletes suffer with what seem to be low grade infections when allergies are at fault. Infections usually run their course and improve with rest. Those that don't may not be infections, but greater sensitivity to common allergens precipitated by the infection.

Those of you who wheeze and have a lot of phlegm after strenuous effort may suffer from exercise-induced asthma. Cold air, allergies, stress, and other factors sometimes cause bronchial passages to constrict, making breathing difficult. Mild cases often respond to a technique called PEEP (Positive End-Expiratory Pressure), which involves exhaling through pressed lips, but many of you will have to resort to medication to relieve the problem. Consult an allergy/asthma specialist for advice.

DRUGS AND DOPING

Whether it be for asthma, allergies, or to relieve the symptoms of the common cold, we all occasionally take some form of medication. Both you and your coach should be aware of the drugs that are prohibited in major international competitions. The anti-doping regulations laid down by the Medical Committee of the International Ski Federation (FIS) call for urine samples following major ski events. In addition to losing a medal, a competitor found with illegal substances in the urine could be banned from future FIS competitions. The current list of substances includes those shown in Table 13.1. Note that the list is subject to change; consult the latest issue of the International Olympic Committee medical controls publication for up-to-date information.

STRESS SYNDROME

How can you tell if you are overtraining or becoming stale? Hans Selye, the famous Canadian researcher, did pioneering work on the subject of stress. He found that a number of stressors such as infection, emotional disturbance, extreme exertion, or exhaustion could lead to a series of reactions in the body. If the stressors were severe enough or if they persisted, the body's resistance would break down.

Stress

Emotional stress can drain enthusiasm and sap energy. We engage in competitive athletics because we enjoy the thrill of stress, but excess stress breaks down resistance. Many life events, both good and bad, contribute to a stress buildup. Too much at one time and you're headed for a burnout. Common causes of stress include the obvious:

- Death in family
- Major illness or injury
- Divorce
- Financial problems
- Trouble at school
- Trouble with the law

Less obvious events, even happy ones, contribute to the stress buildup:

- Holiday
- Vacation
- Change in social or recreational habits

TABLE 13.1   International List of Illegal Substances

Psychomotor Stimulant Drugs	*Sympathomimetic Amines*
Amphetamine	Chlorprenaline
Benzphetamine	Ephedrine
Caffeine*	Etafedrine
Chlophentermine	Isoetharine
Cocaine	Isoprenaline
Diethylpropion	Methoxyphenamine
Dimethylamphetamine	Methylephedrine
Ethylamphetamine	Related compounds
Fencamfamine	
Meclofenoxate	*Miscellaneous Central Nervous System Stimulants*
Methylamphetamine	Amiphenazole
Methylphenidate	Bemigride
Norpseudoephedrine	Doxapram
Pemoline	Ethamivan
Phendimetrazine	Leptazol
Phentermine	Micorene
Pipradol	Nikethamide
Prolintane	Pentylenetetrazol
Related compounds	Picrotoxine
	Strychnine
Narcotic Analgesics	Related compounds
Anileridine	
Codeine	*Anabolic Steroids*
Dextromoramide	Clostebol
Dihydrocodeine	Dehydrochlormethyltestosterone
Dipipanone	Fluoxymesterone
Ethylmorphine	Mesterolone
Heroin	Metenolone
Hydrocodone	Methandienone
Hydromorphone	Methyltestosterone
Levorphanol	Nandrolone
Methadone	Norethandrolone
Morphine	Oxymesterone
Oxocodone	Oxymetholone
Oxomorphone	Stanozolol
Pentazocine	Testosterone*
Pethidine	Related compounds
Phenazozine	
Piminodine	*Alcohol*
Thebacon	
Trimeperidine	
Related compounds	

*Above a level yet to be determined.

- Change in residence or school
- Personal achievement
- Travel

Be alert to these stressors and don't hesitate to make adjustments. Often a change is all you need to reduce the stress. If you're overworked, try a rest; if you're bored during a long vacation, inject a training routine; if the pressure of competition builds up, try a diversion like a ski tour, or downhill skiing; if you experience chronic fatigue, check your diet.

Stress in Skiing

A number of stressors are common to competitive cross-country skiing. They include travel, sleep loss, long races, and living with the same few athletes for extended periods of time. As with other life stressors, they can add up to a level that begins to affect performance, lower resistance, and set the stage for illness or injury. A brief look at each will help you see how you can better manage the stress of competition.

Travel. Travel is stressful in several ways. Passage through several time zones disrupts normal sleep patterns as well as training, eating, and other important routines. The time spent in travel is stressful because we are usually confined in a car or plane, unable to move about. The effects of travel remain, sometimes for days. They should be considered when planning races and practice schedules. Adjust to upcoming travel by shifting gradually to the new time zone. When travel begins, sleep as often as you can in anticipation of eventual sleep disturbance.

Sleep. Sleep loss has a multitude of effects on performance. Not the least of which is its effect on the activity of aerobic (endurance) enzymes. Also, the rapid eye movement (REM) stage of sleep, that stage in which we dream, is important for resting inhibitory neurons. Continued loss of REM sleep leads to neurotic and eventually psychotic behavior. Combined with the effects of travel, sleep loss can ruin a race performance. Vivid proof of its effects occurred during the 1983 World Cup circuit. Russian skier Alexander Zavalov was slightly ahead of Bill Koch when the circuit moved to Alaska. The Russians' late arrival was compounded by plane trouble, and they didn't get in until 6 a.m. on the day before the races. On race day, Koch regained his lead as the Russian athlete struggled to ski in a race that was scheduled during the early morning of his biological clock. Daily rhythms of sleep and hormonal secretions influence performance profoundly. Allow yourself time to adjust or your performance might suffer as much as 5-6%.

Races. Race length can also be a stressor. Short races have short recovery periods, but longer events may require days of recovery. No one should be expected to go out and hammer on the days after a 50-kilometer race. Race difficulty can vary with snow and weather conditions, and a hard 15 km can be more stressful than a fast 30. Therefore, be sure to allow for race difficulty.

Training. High intensity training or long, hard workouts also place extra stress on the system. Again, you need extra recovery time; without it you'll lose your zip and become a candidate for stress illness or injury.

Personal Factors. A multitude of personal factors can affect performance for some athletes. Personal relationships are strained during periods of close living, in training camps and during extended travel, for example. Athlete-athlete, coach-athlete, and family-athlete relationships can go sour, draining enthusiasm and energy. Bad living accommodations or poor quality or quantity of food will also make training and racing more difficult. Athletes and coaches should recognize how these factors affect performance and do all they can to minimize conflicts, complaints, and the resulting tension and stress. Use the following scale to gauge the probable effects of combined stressors on performance.

Skiers' Stress Scale

The arbitrary scale shown in Table 13.2 was constructed with the help of Dr. Lew Vadheim to help coaches and athletes assess the cumulative effects of stress. No absolute scale is possible, since each of us perceives stress differently. The scale does illustrate the probable effect of combined stressors on performance. Use it as a guide to plan travel, racing, and training schedules and to minimize the effects of stress on performance. Add the day's stress score to that for the preceding 4 days. Be careful when the daily score exceeds 10 or the 5-day total exceeds 25.

Remember, use rest, light exercise, or diversion to help reduce stress. Or, practice other forms of stress reduction such as meditation (relaxation) or biofeedback. When personal problems become a factor, talk them out with the coach, fellow athletes, or family members.

Overtraining

Be alert to the signs of overtraining, signs you must heed if you intend to make steady progress in training. Simple measures such as resting pulse, body weight, and oral temperature can indicate overtraining or impending infection (see Table 13.3). Rest at the right time could save a lot of lost practice time. Other obvious signs such as

TABLE 13.2   Skiers' Stress Scale

	1 Day After	2 Days After	3 Days After	4 Days After	5 Days After
Training/Racing					
Training—length/intensity up to 3 points for long/hard	3	2	1	—	—
Racing—length/difficulty up to 5 points for long/hard	5	4	3	2	1
Travel					

Hours of travel
    1 point for each 4 hours
    (up to 5 points)
	5	4	3	2	1

Time zones
    1 point for each 2 zones
    (up to 5 points)
	5	4	3	2	1

Travel difficulty—delays, etc. up to 3 points	3	2	1	—	—
Personal Factors					

Sleep loss
    1 point for each 2 hours
    (up to 4 points)
	4	3	2	1	—

Food/fluid up to 3 points when poor	3	2	1	—	—
Housing up to 2 points off when poor	2	1	—	—	—
Personal relationships up to 5 points off when poor	5	4	3	2	1

Illness/injury
    up to 3 points off upon
    return to training
	3	2	1	—	—

Note that the effects of travel, sleep loss, and other sources of stress persist for several days. Be sure to include these points in the next day's total and in the 5-day total.

minor injuries can foretell impending exhaustion. So don't be afraid to listen to your body, and accept what it says. If you feel too tired to practice—don't. If you're not up to a long, hard workout, take an easy one. You have to be able to communicate these feelings. A good coach will listen and understand.

Physiologists are experimenting with more sophisticated indicators of overtraining. White blood cell counts indicate infection. Hemoglobin or other blood measures show fatigue. Lactic acid levels show how hard a workout was, and certain enzymes in the blood indicate muscle breakdown. These and other measures may be available to competitors on the Olympic team, but they're not essential. Your body has a way of telling you when to rest, just listen to it.

TABLE 13.3   Overtraining Indices

Index	How It's Used
Pulse index	Take your pulse rate daily (for 60 seconds) in the morning before you arise. Average the daily rates. When the morning pulse is 5 or more beats above the average you should suspect overtraining or illness.
Temperature index	Take your morning temperature daily for a week to establish your "normal," then use it whenever the morning pulse is elevated. A fever usually indicates infection. Take the day off.
Weight index	Take your weight daily, in the morning (after toilet but before breakfast). Average daily weights. A rapid or persistent weight loss could indicate impending problems due to: poor eating habits, failure to replace fluids, nervousness, or excessive fatigue.
Fluid index	At the end of the day rate your fluid intake. Failure to replace fluids could lead to dehydration exhaustion. 5—much above average 4—above average 3—average 2—below average 1—much below average
Sleep index	Every morning for a week rate the quality of your sleep; consider ease of falling asleep, quality of sleep, amount of sleep. A persistent drop in quality or quantity calls for a rest. 5—much above average 4—above average 3—average 2—below average 1—much below average
Fatigue index	In the morning, after you arise, rate your tiredness. Persistent fatigue calls for a rest. 9—ready to drop 8—extremely tired 7—very tired 6—slightly tired 5—about average 4—somewhat fresh 3—very fresh 2—extremely fresh 1—full of life

Other useful signs include color of urine (dark, concentrated or cloudy?); skin color (pasty, pale, gray); pain or weakness in joints. Try the indices for 2 weeks, then use those that work best for you.

Cross-country skiing isn't another 3-month involvement, it is a life-time sport. So don't sacrifice long-term goals to achieve immediate success. Success comes to those who pace themselves. Some burn brightly and then fade, others are in the race until the end, practicing good judgment, self-discipline, and moderation.

SUMMARY

Although most of this book has focused on the physiology of training for cross-country ski racing, I would not want to leave you with the impression that physiology is all that matters. Cross-country presents an immense physical challenge, but it offers intense psychological, emotional, and sometimes spiritual rewards as well. Many skiers are attracted by the physical challenge. Others come for phychological reasons and grow to enjoy the physical ones. And many remain to experience each level of involvement as they mature with the sport. A well-designed training program makes skiing easier and opens the senses to the many dimensions of cross-country. I hope this book helps you to better understand your body and how it adapts to training, and thereby derive even greater enjoyment from participation in skiing and ski racing.

Epilogue

People often wonder about the future of cross-country ski racing in this country. How can we attract and keep the best athletes in this demanding sport? Can we test boys and girls so we can identify those with the potential to make the Olympic team a decade later? We could put our top skiers through a battery of lab tests including maximal oxygen intake, strength, power, speed, agility, balance, and body fat. We could do muscle biopsies to determine fiber types and muscle enzyme levels. Blood tests would yield information about red cells, hemoglobin, and iron. With this information and more we could then develop a profile of the world class skier and use that profile as a model for the future. Unfortunately, we could be wrong.

In the early 1970s the Finns began a systematic testing program involving many of the items listed above. Surprisingly, that profile has changed somewhat over the last 10 years. In other words, the top skiers today have slightly different characteristics than the top skiers of the 70s. Why? Because cross-country skiing has changed. In the 1970s skiers from the Soviet Union battled their way to prominence using power instead of style and grace. In 1974 fiberglass skis kicked off an equipment revolution that is still in progress. Lighter, faster skis were followed by improved boot binding systems, better poles, and skin-tight racing suits. Improved track setting and grooming machines, combined with lighter and more maneuverable ski equipment, called for more challenging courses, involving difficult uphill and downhill sections to better test technique. So the skier chosen in the early 70s might not be the best for the 80s.

But, you may say, the equipment revolution is over; now we can use today's skier to predict the champion of the future. Don't assume too much; even though the hectic evolution of equipment seems to be slowing down, and even if courses and waxes remain the same, there is no reason to assume that the sport will remain static (witness the controversial introduction of the marathon skate by Bill Koch and its effect on the sport). An analysis of world running records for short to long distances indicates a steady progress over many decades. There is no evidence that runners have even begun to approach their physiological limits. The authors of a study reported in the prestigious *Scientific American* (Ryder, Carr, and Herget, 1976) suggest that current limits are influenced by how much time an athlete is willing and able to spend in training.

With more and more skiers spending more time training, the same will be true for cross-country skiing. Just as "distance" races like the mile run are now classified as middle distance, the 10 km ski race may some day be a sprint. Today's athletes skate the flats, run up hills, and double pole down; someday the classic diagonal stride may become a pleasant memory of days past. Preposterous? Maybe, but we can never predict changes yet to be made, or the sacrifices athletes will make to become internationally competitive.

Does that mean that we shouldn't try to recruit the best athletes for cross-country? On the contrary, we should, but we also have a responsibility to do the best for all who elect to make cross-country their sport. In his book, *In Pursuit of Excellence*, Orlick (1980) points out the importance of personal commitment for success in any sport. We need athletes who are willing to work long and hard to achieve personal excellence. In that group there will always be a few who prove the lab tests inadequate, who—because of hard work, late maturity, or sheer persistence—achieve success no one ever expected.

You may have noticed that cross-country ski racing doesn't always attract or keep the most gifted young athletes. Cross-country must compete with a number of sports considered more important or glamorous because of the emphasis placed on these sports in the schools. Hardly a week goes by that I don't hear about a fine skier who has put his or her skis aside to accept a scholarship in another sport. School programs in many states are poorly funded, and tight budgets are causing some states to drop high school programs. College programs are also suffering. Since budgets aren't likely to improve in the near future and since ski coaches are seldom found in positions of power in state or college athletic associations, one answer to the problem is to return to the club system which serves cross-country so well in other countries. This country's success in swimming is based on large numbers of kids in community swim clubs. Start large numbers of youngsters out in junior programs, and keep as many involved for as long as possible. You may lose kids to other sports, but if the program is good and enjoyable, many will come back. In my view the answer isn't to pick a chosen few, but rather to get all the kids you can involved in what some of us think is the greatest sport of all.

The Cross-Country Skiing Fitness Test

A series of simple field tests designed to:

- Encourage off-season training
- Recognize effort and accomplishment
- Identify potential talent
- Promote the further development of cross-country skiing

Test items include:

- Percent body fat (skinfold calipers)
- Flexibility (sit and reach)
- Abdominal tone (curl-ups)
- Power (stair run)
- Aerobic fitness (1½ mile run)
- Arm strength/power (roller board test)

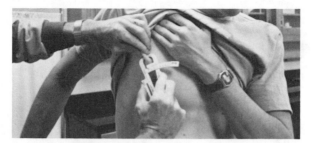

Figure A.1   Inexpensive skinfold calipers available from Ross Laboratories, Columbus, Ohio, allow accurate estimations of percent body fat.

TEST INSTRUCTIONS

1. Body Fat

Use the skinfold calipers (see Figure A.1) and nomogram to determine percent body fat.

- Take all measures on right side of body
- Grasp skinfold between thumb and forefinger
- Place calipers on as far as fold is wide
- Squeeze calipers to align lines
- Read skinfold in millimeters
- Remove calipers from fold
- Repeat until you get a consistent measure

Chest. Above and to side of chest (Figure A.2). Don't get muscle in the skinfold.

Abdomen. On level of umbilicus (Figure A.3). Don't put your finger in the belly button.

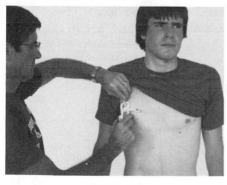

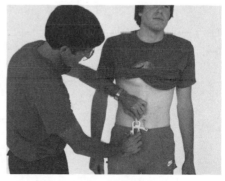

Figure A.2   **Figure A.3**

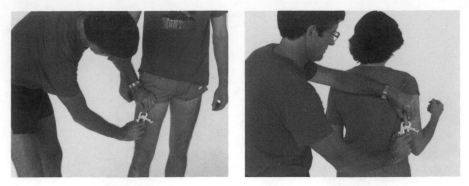

Figure A.4   **Figure A.5**

Thigh. Athlete stands with weight on left leg, right leg relaxed. Take fold on front of thigh (Figure A.4).

Triceps. Back of arm, midway between shoulder and elbow (Figure A.5).

Thigh. As for males.

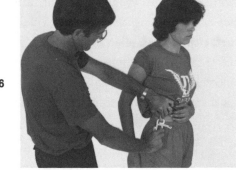

Figure A.6

Suprailium. Above iliac crest (hip) on side of body (Figure A.6). Locate top of hip and take fold just above the bone.

Then add the three skinfolds and use Figure A.7 to determine percent of body fat.

Fitness Test Evaluation

1. Body Fat (%)

	Bronze	Silver	Gold
Men	14 - 17	10 - 13	5 - 9
Women	22 - 24	18 - 21	12 - 17

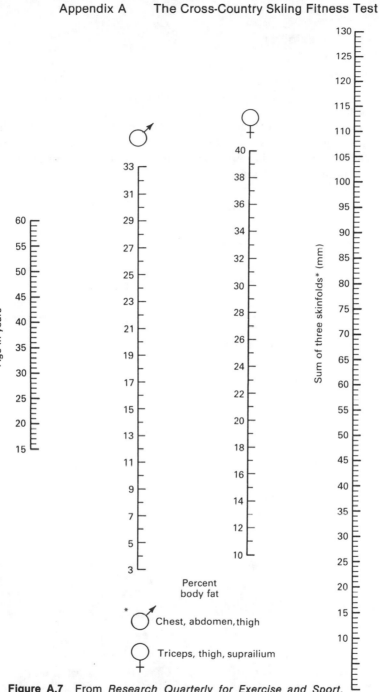

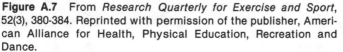

Figure A.7 From *Research Quarterly for Exercise and Sport*, 52(3), 380-384. Reprinted with permission of the publisher, American Alliance for Health, Physical Education, Recreation and Dance.

2. Flexibility

Sit and Reach
EQUIPMENT. Mat or rug and a 12 or 18" ruler.
DIRECTIONS. Subject sits with legs *flat* on mat. After two warm-up trials the subject reaches as far as possible and holds for several seconds (one hand on top of other). Test administrator holds ruler so number 6 is above toes. Score is number of inches (+ or −) reached on third trial. Administrator should be sure legs are flat and toes point up (see Figure A.8).

Fitness Test Evaluation

2. Flexibility (inches)

	Bronze	Silver	Gold
Men	− 3 - − 1	0 - 2	3 +
Women	− 1 - + 2	3 - 5	6 +

3. Abdominal Tone

Curl-ups
EQUIPMENT. Mat or rug and a stopwatch. Optional equipment includes padded board with strap for testing and training (use as a tiltboard for training).
DIRECTIONS. Subject lies on back with knees flexed, heels 12-18 inches from buttocks, arms folded across chest with hands on opposite shoulders and chin tucked to chest. Assistant holds subject's feet down (Figure A.9). On command of *begin*, the subject curls up until elbows touch legs, then returns to starting position. Chin remains tucked to chest. Each curl-up counts as one repetition. The score is the

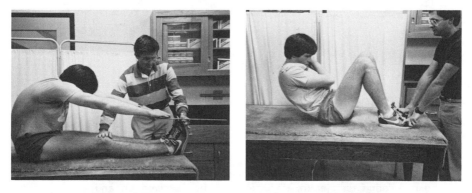

Figure A.8   Figure A.9

total number completed in 60 seconds (repetitions are not counted when hands do not remain on the shoulders or when the elbows come off the chest). The back should touch the mat before the next curl-up is performed.

Fitness Test Evaluation

3. Abdominal Tone (Curl-Up Repetitions)

	Bronze	Silver	Gold
Men	50 - 54	55 - 59	60 +
Women	45 - 49	50 - 54	55 +

4. Power

Stair Run Test

EQUIPMENT. Stopwatch that records to hundredths of a second; flight of stairs with 7- or 8-inch rise per step (Figure A.10). After slow practice trials, subject runs 10-foot approach and runs up stairs—two at a time—as fast as possible. Administrator times run between steps 2 and 10. Subject takes several trials; time is average of best two trials.

SCORING.

$$\text{Speed} = \frac{\text{vertical feet}}{\text{time}} = \text{vertical ft/sec}$$

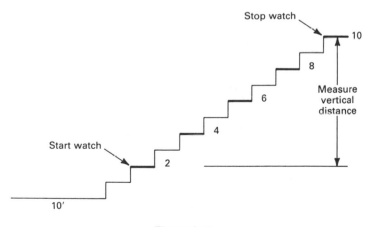

Figure A.10

Fitness Test Evaluation

4. Power (Stair Run—ft/sec)

	Bronze	Silver	Gold
Men	5 - 5.5	5.5 - 6.0	Over 6.0
Women	4.75 - 5.25	5.25 - 5.75	Over 5.75

5. Aerobic Fitness

1.5-Mile Run. Before the run, go through a light warmup, then rest. Run the 1½ miles over a level course. Pacing and high motivation are essential for best performance. Use your time for the run to predict aerobic fitness and work capacity. If you've been inactive, precede the test with at least 8 weeks of training (walk-jog-run program). Those over 35 years of age should have a medical examination, including an exercise electrocardiogram (see Figure A.11).

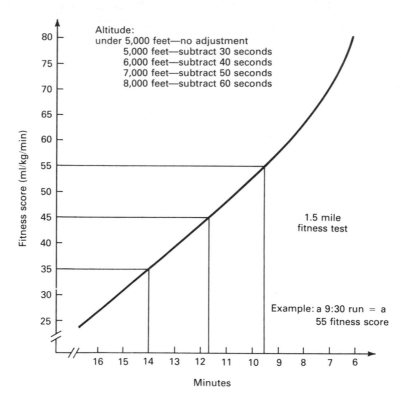

Figure A.11

Fitness Test Evaluation

5. Aerobic Fitness (ml/kg/min)

	Bronze	Silver	Gold
Men	60 - 64	65 - 69	70 +
Women	53 - 57	58 - 62	63 +

6. Arm Strength/Power

Roller Board Test

EQUIPMENT. 10-foot roller board (see Appendix F) set so the bottom of the front lower edge is *36* inches above the ground (see Figure A.12). Board is marked at 4 and 8 feet and secured to prevent wobble. See Figure A.13 for details and Figure E.1 for construction diagram.

DIRECTIONS. On freshly waxed roller board, adjust length of arm pulls and give subject several practice trials as administrator instructs on proper form (keep arms relatively straight, pull up to mark

Figure A.12

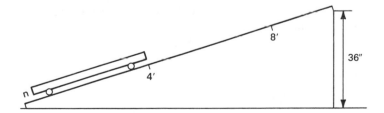

Figure A.13   Construction details for rollerboard in Appendix E.

on board). After a brief rest the subject then does as many complete trials as possible at a set rhythm (pull up on second 1, down on 2 and 3, or 20 per minute). A complete trial is when subject pulls up to mark and returns to starting point. Test stops when subject cannot continue or is unable to maintain rhythm. Score is number of complete repetitions.

Fitness Test Evaluation

6. Arm Strength/Power (Repetitions)

	Bronze	Silver	Gold
Men	30 - 34	35 - 39	40 +
Women	25 - 29	30 - 34	35 +

ADDITIONAL TESTS

Additional tests can be used to determine other important components of cross-country skiing. Since these components cannot be standardized the scores only have meaning when compared with others on the same course.

Anaerobic Capacity

30-Second Hill Run: On a relatively steep hill (a grade greater than 10%) select and mark a course with good footing that can be used from year to year. After a good warm-up, have athletes run uphill as fast as possible for 30 seconds. The score is the distance covered. An alternative method of administration is to have athletes run a given distance and record the time, which should be about 30 seconds long. Test in the off season and strive for improvement in subsequent weeks and months of training.

Aerobic Power

2-Mile Hill Run: Select a long hill with a relatively consistent grade (6-10%) and good footing. After a warm-up, have athletes run the 2-mile course as fast as possible. Record the time in the off season and test again in the fall to see the effects of vertical training.

Establish additional tests such as:

- Aerobic fitness of arms (1½ mile double pole on roller skiis)
- Arm strength (dips, Nautilus pull-overs)
- Arm endurance (push-ups)

Cross-Country
Skiing Questionnaire

Complete the questionnaire to determine gaps in your training program. Take it again 6 months later to see if you've filled in these gaps. Then take it once a year to see how training changes. Use different colored pencils each time.

NORDIC SPORTSMEDICINE PROGRAM

TRAINING FOR CROSS COUNTRY SKI RACING

A questionnaire distributed by the U.S. Ski Team Nordic Sportsmedicine Council to identify and improve training programs for skiers of all ages.

Name _____ Citizen of _____

Today's Date _____ Ski Race _____

Sex _____ Age _____ Height _____ Weight _____

	0-1 Years	2-4	5-6	7 or Over
Years Cross Country Skiing	☐	☐	☐	☐
Years Cross Country Racing	☐	☐	☐	☐
Years Other Skiing Alpine	☐	☐	☐	☐
Nordic/Downhill	☐	☐	☐	☐

Are you affiliated with an organized racing program or club? Yes_____ No_____

Other current competitive endurance sports involvements:

Running ☐   Cycling ☐   Other _____

Swimming ☐   Rowing ☐   Other _____

TRAINING

Years of Training for Cross Country Skiing	0-1 Years ☐	2-3 ☐	4-5 ☐	6 or Over ☐	
Months Per Year Devoted to Cross Country Ski Training	0-3 Months ☐	4-6 ☐	7-9 ☐	10-12 ☐	
Current Average Hours of Training Per Week	4-6/Week ☐	7-9 ☐	10-12 ☐	13-15 ☐	16+ ☐
Compared to Last Year, That is	More ☐	Same ☐	Less ☐		

Average Off-season (Dry Land) Training (Hours Per Week)

	0 Hrs./Week	1-2	3-4	5-6	7 or More
Running	☐	☐	☐	☐	☐
Hiking	☐	☐	☐	☐	☐
Ski Stride (With Poles)	☐	☐	☐	☐	☐
Roller Ski	☐	☐	☐	☐	☐
Bicycle	☐	☐	☐	☐	☐
Other _____	☐	☐	☐	☐	☐

Average Off-season (Dry Land) Training (Hours Per Week)

	0	1-2	3-4	5-6	7 or More
Over Distance	☐	☐	☐	☐	☐
Vertical (Hills)	☐	☐	☐	☐	☐
Fartlek (Speed Play)	☐	☐	☐	☐	☐
Speed (Sprints)	☐	☐	☐	☐	☐
Intervals	☐	☐	☐	☐	☐
Pace (Race Pace)	☐	☐	☐	☐	☐
Other _____	☐	☐	☐	☐	☐

	Under 500 Feet/Week	500-1000	1000-2000	2000-3000	Over 3000
Average Off-season Weekly Vertical	☐	☐	☐	☐	☐

Roller Ski Training Includes (Hours Per Week)

	0	1-2	3-4	5-6	7 or More
Arms Only	☐	☐	☐	☐	☐
Arms and Legs	☐	☐	☐	☐	☐

Bicycle Training Includes (Hours Per Week)

	0	1-2	3-4	5-6	7 or More
Seated	☐	☐	☐	☐	☐
Standing	☐	☐	☐	☐	☐

Off Season Muscular Fitness Training Includes (Check)

	High Resistance Low Repititions	Med Resistance Med Repititions	Low Resistance High Repititions
Free Weights	☐	☐	☐
Weight Machine	☐	☐	☐
Roller Board	☐	☐	☐
Exercisor (Exergenie Apollo, Bands)	☐	☐	☐
Other _____	☐	☐	☐

	0 Hours/ Week	1-2	3-4	5-6	7 or Over
Average Off-season Muscular Training Fitness	☐	☐	☐	☐	☐

PRE AND EARLY SEASON TRAINING

Number of Pre-season Training Camps Attended Each Year	0 ☐	1-2 ☐	3 or More ☐		
Total Number of Days in Training Camps	0-4 Days ☐	5-9 ☐	10-14 ☐	15-19 ☐	20 or More ☐

Typical Training Altitude .... Feet _____ or Meters _____

	No	Up to 2500' Higher	2500-5000' Higher	Over 5000' Higher	
Do You Race at a Higher Elevation?	☐	☐	☐	☐	

	0-1 Days	2-5	6-10	11-15	Over 15
If Yes, How Many Days in Advance of the Race Do You Train at the Higher Elevation?	☐	☐	☐	☐	☐

Do You Train at Higher Elevations Then Come Down to Race?   Yes ☐   No ☐

If Yes, Do You Feel You Gain an
Advantage in Performance? ......Performance Improves ☐   No Benefit ☐   Performance Suffers ☐

RACING AND PERFORMANCE

	0-2 Races	3-5	7-9	Over 10	
Typical Number of Ski Races Per Season ...	☐	☐	☐	☐	

	Under 10 km	10-15	20-30	50 or Over	
Check All Distances You Race	☐	☐	☐	☐	

	0-50 km	51-100	100-150	150-200	Over 200
Total Number of Kilometers Raced Per Season	☐	☐	☐	☐	☐

	Under 30 Minutes	30-35	35-40	40-45	Over 45
Best Time in a 10 km Race	☐	☐	☐	☐	☐

or	Under 3				
Average Time Per km	Minutes	3-3.5	3.5-4	4-4.5	Over 4.5
(Race Length _____ km)	☐	☐	☐	☐	☐

Did You Attempt to Peak for Important Races?   Yes ☐   No ☐

	0-2 Weeks	3-4	5-6	Over 6	
If Yes, How Long Can You Maintain the Peak?	☐	☐	☐	☐	

Non-snow Training During Season (Hours Per Week)	0	1-2	3-4	5-6	7 or More
Running	☐	☐	☐	☐	☐
Roller Skiing	☐	☐	☐	☐	☐
Weights	☐	☐	☐	☐	☐
Other _____.	☐	☐	☐	☐	☐

C

Weekly
Training Log

Season _____ Week of _____ - _____ Name _____

Day	Energy Training			Muscular Fitness					Body Wt.	A.M. Pulse
		Hrs.	Exercises	Wt.	Reps	Plyometrics	Other	Flexibility		
Mon.	A.M.									
	P.M.									
Tues.	A.M.									
	P.M.									
Wed.	A.M.			Wt.	Reps					
	P.M.									
Thurs.	A.M.									
	P.M.									
Fri.	A.M.			Wt.	Reps					
	P.M.									
Sat.										
Sun.										

Weekly goal _____ hrs.   Total hrs. _____

Comments

D

Dry-Land Training Techniques

These techniques are classified according to their contribution to muscular fitness, energy training, and oxygen transport, and for their specificity to skiing muscles.

Figure D.1 Roller skates can be used to train skating muscles.

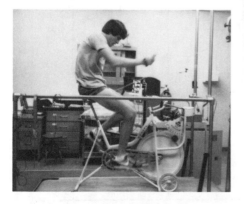

Figure D.2 Combined arm and leg exercise loads the oxygen transport system.

	Muscular Fitness	Energy Training	Oxygen Transport	Ski Specific
Arms				
Weights and weight machines	****	*	—	*
Exergenie and Nordic track	**	**	*	**
Paddling	**	***	**	*
Roller board	**	*	*	**
Roller ski (arms)	*	***	**	***
Legs				
Weights and weight machines	****	*	*	*
Plyometrics	**	*	*	**
Cycle (some standing)	**	***	***	***
Hiking/striding	**	**	**	**
Skating	**	*	*	**
Roller ski (legs)	**	**	**	***
Running (some hills)	**	****	****	***
Combined				
Rowing	**	***	***	*
Cycle & exergenie	**	***	****	**
Ski mill/Ski lmit	*	***	****	***
Ski stride/bound	**	****	****	***
Skate with poles	*	***	***	***
Sand or grass ski	**	**	***	**
Roller skiing	*	****	****	****

*Fair   **Good   ***Very good   ****Excellent

Energy training and oxygen transport depend on intensity and duration of effort.

Figure D.3 Ski striding.

E

Back Yard Training Center

Our training center includes a roller board (see Figures E.1, E.2) and a sit-up board as well as stations for basket hang (and chin-ups) (Figure

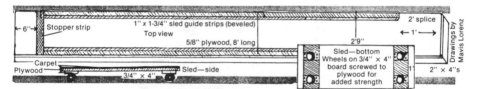

Figure E.1 Roller board. Drawing by Mavis Lorenz.

Figure E.2

E.3), an exergenie (Figure E.4), back-ups (Figure E.5), and parallel bars for arm work. It was built with scrap lumber for about $30. Design one to suit your needs. (For construction ideas see *Fitness Trail*, c/o USDA/Forest Service, Missoula Equipment Development Center, Bldg. #1, Fort Missoula, Missoula, MT 59801.)

Figure E.3   **Figure E.4**

Figure E.5

F

Muscular Fitness Exercises

This section provides exercise suggestions to help you achieve flexibility, strength, endurance, and power. The strength, endurance, and power exercises are arranged according to the part of the body involved: arms and shoulders; trunk; legs. In order to develop your muscular fitness program follow the steps listed below:

1. List seasonal goals (strength, endurance, or power).
2. Determine your individual needs (e.g., upper body strength).
3. Identify muscle groups involved.
4. Select specific exercises.

Example: In off season a skier can build up strength. The junior skier needs strength for poling, skating, etc. For arms and shoulders: work on pullovers and tricep; for the trunk: work on abdominal curls and back-ups; for the legs: work on the leg press, toe raises, and hamstring/gluteal exercises.

Unless you have lots of time to spend on muscular fitness training you should select the most important muscle groups and do the exercises regularly. Follow the training prescriptions listed in Chapter 9 to achieve results. Once you have adequate strength in the major muscle groups used in skiing you can worry about training the lesser used or accessory muscles.

FLEXIBILITY USING ON-SKI STRETCHING EXERCISE

Use a few basic stretching exercises before or after a few minutes of road or snow skiing.

Stride Stretch

For arms and shoulders and leg (groin) muscles. Hold 5-10 seconds, then switch sides. Also use the inside thigh stretch to relieve early season soreness.

Bent Knee Stretch

For lower back and hamstrings. Grasp ankles and pull until you feel the stretch.

ADDITIONAL FLEXIBILITY EXERCISES

Use these exercises as needed to avoid injury or relieve soreness.

1. Toe Pull

For groin and thighs. Pull on toes while pressing legs down with elbows.

Variation: Lean forward and try to touch head to feet or floor.

2. Seated Toe Touch

For back and hamstrings. With toes pointed, slide hands down legs until you feel stretch. Hold for five counts and relax. Now grasp ankles and pull until head approaches legs. Relax. Draw toes back and slowly attempt to touch toes.

Variation: Try with legs apart.

3. Leg Pull

For hamstrings and gluteals. Pull leg toward and across chest, feeling the stretch high in hamstring. Hold for five counts and relax.

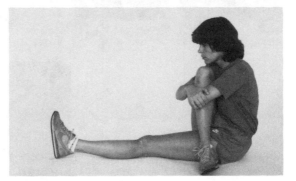

4. Backover

For hamstrings and low back. Starting with knees bent, bring legs over head and try to touch floor with toes until you feel stretch. Hold, relax.

5. Stride Stretch

For inside thigh muscles (groin). Assume stride position with hands on floor or chair for balance. Feel the stretch, hold, and relax. Put arm and shoulder inside front leg to accentuate stretch.

6. Side Stretch

For arms and trunk. Grasp hands above head and slowly bend to one side. Bob gently, hold, and relax. Switch sides.

7. Wall Stretch

For calves and Achilles tendon. Stand about three feet from wall, feet slightly apart. Lean forward, keep heels on floor, and feel stretch in calves.

Variation: Concentrate on one leg at a time. Contract calf muscle briefly; then relax and feel stretch in Achilles tendon.

8. Shoulder Stretch

Pull arms back until partner feels stretch. Hold, relax.

9. Back and Leg Stretch

Pull on ankles to feel stretch in lower back, hamstrings, and buttocks (gluteals).

Variation: In time you may be able to touch fingers or palms to the floor.

10. The Bow

For arms, back, legs. Bow at waist. Put hands on wall and feel stretch from hands to heels.

Other Exercises

1. Side twist—with arms extended to side, twist back and forth slowly to stretch trunk.
2. Neck circles—gently roll head in full circle, first to one side, then the other.
3. The hug—hug yourself as tightly as possible to stretch shoulders.

Do other exercises as indicated by tightness or soreness.

MUSCULAR FITNESS EXERCISE SUGGESTIONS FOR THE ARMS AND SHOULDERS

1. Bench Press
For chest and tricep muscles.

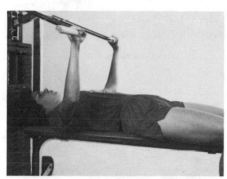

Universal.

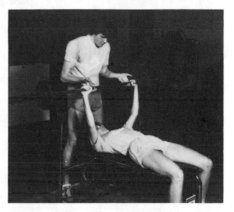

Free weights. (Be sure to use a spotter.)

Nautilus.

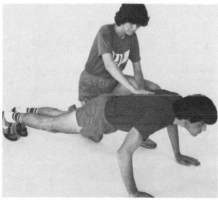

Counterforce. Resisted push-ups load the same muscle groups.

2. Lateral Pull

For latissimus muscles.

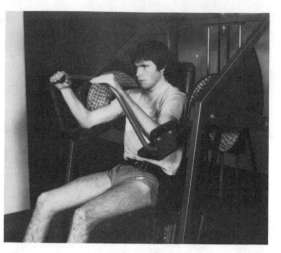

Universal. Modified for
cross-country (towel).

Nautilus. Pull-over.

3. Military Press

For triceps and deltoids.

Universal.

Nautilus.

Other choices: free weights; inverted push-ups.

4. Curls

For biceps (to balance emphasis on triceps).

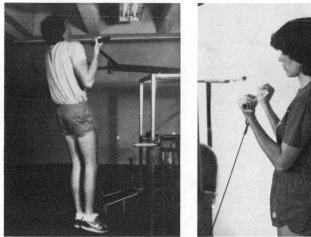

Chin-up.   Universal.

Nautilus.

Also: free weights; mini gym; counterforce. The mini gym can be used for a wide range of ski-specific exercises, including the double pole.

5. Tricep

Calisthenics: Dip. Also back muscles.

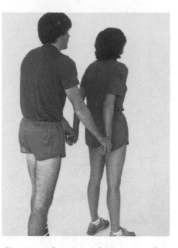

Counterforce. Also posterior deltoid.

Nautilus.
Also: free weights or universal lat station.

6. Deltoid

Nautilus.
Also: free weights; counterforce.

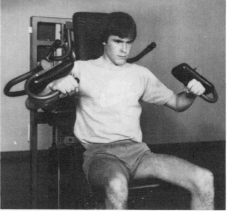

7. Chest

Nautilus.
Also: free weights.

8. Bent Rowing

For upper back, arms, and shoulders (deltoid). Free weights. Pull weight to chest.

9. Shrugs

For shoulders, trapezius muscles. Hold barbell (or handles of Universal bench press) with straight arms. Elevate weight by shrugging shoulders. Roll shoulders in circles from front to back.

Do other exercises as desired to develop balance, symmetry, or to correct a weakness.

MUSCULAR FITNESS EXERCISES
FOR THE TRUNK
1. Abdominals

Calisthenics: basket hang. Pull
knees to chest.

Universal: sit-up. Arms folded
across chest.

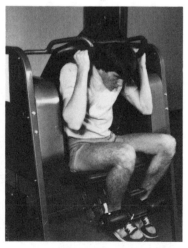

Universal: leg-lift with bent knees.

Weights: sit-ups with weights.

Nautilus.

2. Back

Calisthenics: back up Raise up until abdomen is off mat. Do not hyperextend.

Nautilus. For hamstrings and lower back muscles. Again, avoid hyperextension.

Also: Universal (back up); calisthenics (leg raise): lie on stomach while partner holds shoulders down; lift legs.

3. Side Bends

Free weights. Grasp dumbbell in one hand, hold at side. Bend to that side to lower weight, then lift by bending to other side. Do both sides.

Universal. As above, using arm of bench press machine.

MUSCULAR FITNESS EXERCISES FOR THE LEGS

1. Quads

Universal: leg press.

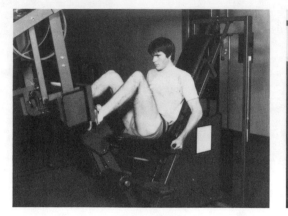

Nautilus: leg extension.   Mini gym leaper.

Free weights: squats (to 90° bend only); always use a spotter.

2. Hamstrings

Nautilus: leg flexion.

Also: Universal; counterforce (partner provides resistance).

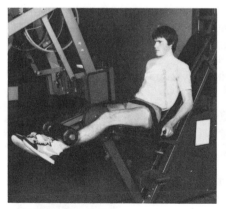

3. Extensors

Nautilus.

Also: Universal; free weights.

4. Adductors (Inside Thigh)

Nautilus.

Also: counterforce; pulley weights.

5. Abductors (Outside of Thigh and Hip)

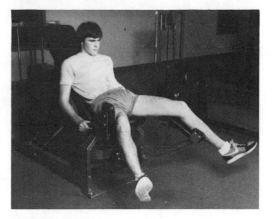

Nautilus.
Also: counterforce; pulley weights.

6. Calf Muscles

Do toe raises with weight on shoulder. Use toes on leg press (Universal or Nautilus) with straight legs.

7. Front Calf (Tibialis Anterior)

Counterforce: pull toe toward shin with resistance.
Weights: drape weighted bags (sand) on toes and lift toes.

PLYOMETRICS

Always do plyos on grass.

1. Indian Hops

Hop high in air, land on jumping foot and then hop off again with the other. Do 15 on each leg, rest, repeat.
Variation: Do up a modest hill.

2. Two-leg Jumps

Blast off with both legs, land, coil, and go again. Do 15, rest, repeat.

3. One-leg Jumps

Drive off one leg at a time; land on the other foot. Gather and go again. Do 15 on each leg, rest, repeat.

Variation: See how far you go in 30 jumps.

4. Down Jumping

Jump down, land on both feet, coil quickly, and blast off. Do 10, rest, repeat.

Caution: Begin on a low box after several weeks of other plyos. Slowly increase height of down jump, but never exceed 30 inches. This is not for young or inexperienced athletes. Stop if knees get sore.

Glossary

Acclimatization — Adaptation to an environmental condition such as heat or altitude.

Accommodating resistance — Resistance adjusts to meet the changing force capabilities of the contracting muscle as in isokinetic (same speed) contractions.

Actin — Muscle protein that works with the protein myosin to produce movement.

Adipose tissue — Tissue in which fat is stored.

Aerobic — In the presence of oxygen; aerobic metabolism utilizes oxygen.

Aerobic capacity — Maximal oxygen intake in liters per minute.

Aerobic fitness — Maximum ability to take in, transport, and utilize oxygen.

Aerobic power — Maximal oxygen intake in milliters per kilogram of body weight per minute.

Agility — Ability to change direction quickly while maintaining control of the body.

Alveoli — Tiny air sacs in the lungs where O_2 and CO_2 exchange takes place.

Amino acids — Form proteins; different arrangements of the 22 amino acids form the various proteins (muscles, enzymes, hormones, etc.).

Anaerobic — In the absence of oxygen, non-oxidation metabolism.

Anaerobic threshold — When aerobic metabolism no longer supplies all the need for energy, energy is produced anaerobically; indicated by increase in lactic acid.

ATP—Adenosine Triphosphate—high energy compound formed from oxidation of fat and carbohydrate. Used as energy supply for muscle and other body functions; the energy currency.

Atrophy—Loss of size of muscle; when muscle isn't used it doesn't turn to fat, it atrophies.

Balance—Ability to maintain equilibrium while in motion.

Blood pressure—Force exerted against the walls of arteries.

Bronchiole—Small branch of airway; sometimes undergoes spasm making breathing difficult, as in exercise induced bronchospasm (EIB).

Buffer—Substance in blood that soaks up hydrogen ions to minimize changes in acid-base balance (pH).

Calories—Amount of heat required to raise one kilogram of water one degree centigrade (same as kilocalorie).

Capillaries—Smallest blood vessels (between arterioles and venules) where oxygen, foods, and hormones are delivered to tissues and carbon dioxide and wastes are picked up.

Carbohydrate—Simple (e.g., sugar) and complex (potatoes, rice, beans, corn grains) foodstuff that we use for energy; stored in liver and muscle as glycogen—excess is stored as fat.

Carbohydrate loading (glycogen loading)—A procedure that elevates muscle glycogen stores.

Cardiac—Pertaining to the heart.

Cardiac output—Volume of blood pumped by the heart each minute; product of heart rate and stroke volume.

Cardiorespiratory endurance—Synonymous with aerobic fitness or maximal oxygen intake.

Cardiovascular system—Heart and blood vessels.

Central nervous system (CNS)—The brain and spinal cord.

Cholesterol—Fatty substance formed in nerves and other tissues. Excessive amounts in blood have been associated with increased risk of heart disease.

Concentric contraction—Shortening of the muscle during contraction.

Constant resistance—Resistance doesn't change, as in weight lifting.

Contraction—Development of tension by muscle: concentric—muscle shortens; eccentric—muscle is lengthened under tension; static—contraction without change in length.

Coronary arteries—Blood vessels that originate from the aorta and branch out to supply oxygen and fuels to the heart muscle.

Counterforce—Resistance exercises with a partner to provide isokinetic contractions in a technique physical therapists call proprioceptive neuromuscular facilitation.

Creatine phosphate (CP)—Energy-rich compound that backs up ATP in providing energy for muscles.

Dehydration—Loss of essential body fluids.

Diastolic pressure—Lowest pressure exerted by blood in artery; occurs during resting phase (diastole) of heart cycle.

Eccentric contraction — Lengthening of the contracted muscle, as when lowering a heavy weight.

Elastic recoil — Release of elastic energy in a muscular contraction brought about by a brief stretch or preload.

Electrocardiogram (ECG) — A graphic recording of the electrical activity of the heart.

Electrolyte — Solution of ions (sodium, potassium) that conducts electric current.

Electromyogram (EMG) — A recording of the electrical activity that immediately precedes muscular contractions to determine the degree of muscular involvement.

Endurance — The ability to persist, to resist fatigue.

Energy balance — Balance of caloric intake and expenditure.

Enzyme — An organic catalyst that accelerates the rate of chemical reactions.

Epinephrine (Adrenalin) — Hormone from the adrenal medulla and nerve endings of the sympathetic nervous system; secreted during times of stress and to help mobilize energy.

Evaporation — Elimination of body heat when sweat vaporizes on surface of skin. Evaporation of one liter of sweat yields a heat loss of 580 calories.

Exercise — Some apply the term specifically to calisthenics; here it is used to denote any form of physical activity — synonymous with effort exertion, physical activity, etc.

Fartlek — Swedish term meaning speed play; a form of training where participants vary speed according to mood as they run through the countryside.

Fast glycolytic fiber — Fast-twitch muscle fiber with limited oxidative capability, easily fatigued.

Fast oxidative glycolytic fiber — Fast-twitch fiber with oxidative and glycolytic capabilities.

Fat — Important energy source; stored for future use when excess fat, carbohydrate, or protein is ingested.

Fatigue — Diminished work capacity, usually short of true physiological limits. Real limits in short intense exercise due to factors within muscle (muscle, pH, calcium), long duration effort — glycogen depletion, or CNS fatigue due to low blood sugar.

Flexibility — Range of motion through which the limbs or body parts are able to move.

Glucose — Energy source transported in blood; essential energy source for brain and nervous tissue.

Glycogen — Storage form of glucose, found in liver and muscles.

Heart rate — Frequency of contraction, often inferred from pulse rate (expansion of artery resulting from beat of heart).

Heat stress — Temperature-humidity combinations that lead to heat disorders such as heat cramps, heat exhaustion, or heat stroke.

Hemoglobin — Iron-containing compound in red blood cell that forms loose association with oxygen.

Hypoglycemia—Low blood sugar (glucose).

Inhibition—Opposite of excitation in the nervous system.

Insulin—Pancreatic hormone responsible for getting blood sugar into cells.

Interval training—Training method that alternates short bouts of intense effort with periods of active rest.

Ischemia—Lack of blood to specific area like heart muscle.

Isokinetic—Contraction against resistance that is varied to maintain high tension throughout range of motion while speed remains constant.

Isometric—Contraction against immovable object (static contraction).

Isotonic—Contraction against a constant resistance.

Lactic acid—Byproduct of anaerobic glycolysis.

Lean body weight—Body weight minus fat weight.

Maximal oxygen intake (uptake, consumption)—Aerobic fitness. Best single measure of fitness with implications for health; synonymous with cardiorespiratory endurance.

Metabolism—Energy production and utilization processes, often mediated by enzymatic pathways.

Mitochondria—Tiny organelles within cells; site of all oxidative energy production.

Motor area—Portion of cerebral cortex that controls movement.

Motoneuron—Nerve which transmits impulse to muscle fibers.

Motor unit—Motor nerve and the muscle fibers it innervates.

Muscle fiber types—Fast twitch fibers are fast contracting but fast to fatigue; slow twitch fibers contract somewhat slower but are fatigue resistant.

Muscle soreness—Discomfort after exercise.

Muscular fitness—The strength, muscular endurance, and flexibility you need to carry out daily tasks and avoid injury.

Myofibril—Contractile threads of muscle composed of proteins actin and myosin.

Myoglobin—A hemoglobin-like compound in muscle; helps bind oxygen.

Myosin—Muscle protein that works with actin to produce movement.

Neuron—Nerve cell that conducts impulse; the basic unit of the nervous system.

Obesity—Excessive body fat (over 20% for men, over 30% for women).

Overload—A greater load than normally experienced; used to coax a training effect from the body.

Oxygen debt—Recovery oxygen uptake above resting requirements to replace deficit incurred during exercise.

Oxygen deficit—Lack of oxygen in early moments of exercise.

Oxygen intake—Oxygen used in oxidative metabolism.

Perceived exertion—Subjective estimate of exercise difficulty.

Peripheral nervous system—Parts of the nervous system not including the brain and spinal cord.

Preload—see Elastic recoil.

Progressive resistance — Training program in which the resistance is increased as the muscles gain in strength.

Protein — Organic compound formed from amino acids; forms muscle tissue, hormones, enzymes, etc.

Power — The rate of doing work $\frac{(f \times d)}{t}$.

Pulse — Wave that travels down the artery after each contraction of the heart (see heart rate).

Respiration — Intake of oxygen from atmosphere into lungs and then via the blood to the tissues, and exhale of carbon dioxide from tissues to the atmosphere.

Repetition maximum (RM) — The maximum number of times you can lift a given weight (1 RM is the most you can lift one time).

Sarcomere — The contractile unit of the muscle.

Slow-twitch fiber — see Muscle fiber types.

Somatotype — Body types: Ectomorph is linear or thin, mesomorph is muscular, and endomorph is fat.

Speed of movement — Comprised of reaction time — time from stimulus to start of movement, and movement time — time to complete the movement.

Strength — Ability of muscle to exert force.

Stroke volume — Volume of blood pumped from ventricle during each contraction of heart.

Synapse — Junction between neurons.

Systolic pressure — Highest pressure in arteries that results from contraction (systole) of heart.

Tendon — Tough connective tissue that connects muscle to bone.

Testosterone — Male hormone.

Threshold — The minimal level required to elicit a response.

Tonus — Muscle firmness in absence of a voluntary contraction.

Triglycerides — A fat consisting of three fatty acids and glycerol.

Valsalva maneuver — Increased pressure in abdominal and thoracic cavities caused by breath holding and extreme effort.

Variable resistance — Resistance varies as muscle moves through range of motion, as with devices that use cams or oval-shaped pulleys.

Velocity — Rate of movement or speed $\frac{(Distance)}{time}$.

Ventilation — The amount of air moving in and out of the lungs per minute, the product of respiratory frequency (f) and tidal volume (TV).

Ventricle — Chamber of heart that pumps blood to lungs (right ventricle) or to rest of body (left ventricle).

Weight training — Progressive resistance exercise using weight for resistance.

Wind chill — Cooling effect of temperature and wind.

Work — Product of force and distance.

Recommended Reading

CROSS-COUNTRY SKI RACING

Caldwell, J. *Caldwell on Competitive Cross-Country Skiing*. Brattleboro, VT: Stephen Greene Press, 1979.

Caldwell, J., and Brady, M. *Citizen Racing*. Seattle: The Mountaineers, 1982.

Hall, M. with P. Penfold. *One Stride Ahead*. Tulsa: Winchester Press, 1981.

Hixson, E. *The Physician and Sportsmedicine Guide to Cross-Country Skiing*. New York: McGraw-Hill, 1980.

US Ski Association. *Nordic Skiing Competition Guide*. Park City, UT: USSA, published annually.

PHYSIOLOGY

Astrand, P.O., and Rodahl, K. *Textbook of Work Physiology*. New York: McGraw-Hill, 1977.

Bergh, U. *The Physiology of Cross-Country Ski Racing*. Champaign, IL: Human Kinetics Publishers, Inc., 1981.

Mathews, D., and Fox, E. *The Physiological Basis of Physical Education and Athletics*. Philadelphia: W.B. Saunders Co., 1981.

Sharkey, B. *Physiology of Fitness*. Champaign, IL: Human Kinetics Publishers, Inc., 1979.

Wilmore, J. *Athletic Training and Physical Fitness*. Boston: Allyn and Bacon, Inc., 1982.

NUTRITION

Eisenman, P., and Johnson, D. *Coaches Guide to Nutrition and Weight Control.* Champaign, IL: Human Kinetics Publishers, Inc., 1982.

Smith, N. *Food for Sport.* Palo Alto: Bull Publishing Co., 1976.

Reference Notes

Bergh, U. *Cardiorespiratory factors in cross-country ski racing.* Paper presented at the annual meeting of the American College of Sports Medicine, Minneapolis, 1982.

Boileau, R., McKeown, B., and Riner, W. *The influence of cardiovascular and metabolic parameters on arm and leg VO_2 max.* Paper presented at the annual meeting of the American College of Sports Medicine, Miami, 1981.

Haymes, E., Puhl, J., and Temples, T. *Training for cross-country skiing and iron status.* Paper presented at the annual meeting of the American College of Sports Medicine, Montreal, 1983.

Weltman, A., Dickinson, A., and Burns, R. *The lactate breaking point and the development of the individualized training program.* Paper presented at the annual meeting of the American College of Sports Medicine, Minneapolis, 1982.

References

Bergh, U., Knastrup, I.-L., and Ekblom, B. Maximal oxygen uptake during exercise with various combinations of arm and leg work. *J. Appl. Physiol.*, 1976, **41**, 191-196.

Bergh, U. *The Physiology of Cross-Country Ski Racing.* Champaign, IL: Human Kinetics Publishers, Inc., 1982.

Davis, K., Packer, L., and Brooks, G. Biochemical adaptation of mitochondria, muscle and whole-animal respiration to endurance training. *Arch. of Biochem. and Biophys.*, 1981, **209**, 539-554.

Felig, P. Amino Acid metabolism in exercise. In P. Milvy (Ed.), *The Marathon.* New York: New York Academy of Sciences, 1977, 56-63.

Frederick, E. *The Running Body.* Mountain View, CA: World Publishers, 1973.

Heusner, W. The theory of strength development for swimming and other sports. *Natl. Strength and Conditioning Assoc. Jour.*, 1982, **3**, 36-39.

Karlsson, J., Eriksson, A., Forsberg, A., Kallberg, L., and Tesch, R. *The Physiology of Alpine Skiing.* Park City, UT: US Ski Coaches Assoc., 1978.

Orlick, T. *In Pursuit of Excellence.* Champaign, IL: Human Kinetics Publishers, Inc., 1980.

Ryder, H., Carr, H., and Herget, R. Future performance in footracing. *Scientific American*, 1976, **234**, 109-116.

Saltin, B. The interplay between peripheral and central factors in the adaptive response to exercise and training. In P. Milvy (Ed.), *The Marathon.* New York: New York Academy of Sciences, 1977, 224-231.

Secher, N., Ruberg-Larsen, N., Brinkhorst, R., and Bonde-Petersen, F. Maximal oxygen uptake during arm cranking and combined arm plus leg exercise. *J. Appl. Physiol.*, 1974, **36**, 515-518.

Sharkey, B., Jukkala, A., and Herzberg, R. *The Fitness Trail.* Missoula, MT: USDA Forest Service, 1978.

Sharkey, B., and Heidel, B. Physiological tests of cross-country skiers. *J. US Ski Coaches Assoc.*, 1981, **5**, 5-15.

Thys, H., Faraggiana, T., and Margaria, R. Utilization of muscle elasticity in exercise. *J. Appl. Physiol.*, 1972, **32**, 491-494.

Washburn, R., Sharkey, B., Narum, J., and Smith, M. Dryland training for cross-country skiers. *Ski Coach*, 1983, **6**, 9-16.

HACKNEY LIBRARY

BARTON COLLEGE LIBRARY

3 6500 00253 8491

796.93
Sh23t

Sharkey, Brian J.

Training for
cross-country ski
racing

LIBRARY
ATLANTIC CHRISTIAN COLLEGE
WILSON. N. C.